GOLF
The Skills of the Game

GOLF
The Skills of the Game

JOHN STIRLING

THE CROWOOD PRESS

First published in 1985 by
THE CROWOOD PRESS
Ramsbury, Marlborough
Wiltshire SN8 2HE

Reprinted 1986
Paperback edition, 1986
Reprinted 1987, 1989 (twice)

British Library Cataloguing in Publication Data

Stirling, John
  Golf: the skills of the game.
  1. Golf
  I. Title
  796.352'3   GV965

  ISBN 0–946284–26–1 (HB)
        0–946284–88–1 (PB)

Acknowledgements

Action photographs by Ken Lewis

Cover shot by Lawrence Levy

Thanks to Meon-Valley Hotel Golf and Country Club for their assistance
with the demonstration photographs

Line illustrations by Annette Findlay

Series Adviser C.E. Bond, MEd, AdvDipPE, DLC (Hons), Head of
Carnegie School of Physical Education & Human Movement Studies

Typeset by Inforum Typesetting, Portsmouth
Printed in Great Britain by Redwood Burn Ltd, Trowbridge

Contents

John Stirling is Golf Professional at Meon Valley Hotel Golf and Country Club. After starting out as an amateur in Scotland, he turned professional in 1951. He played the tournament circuit for many years, before concentrating on teaching. He is National Coach to the English Golf Union, Senior Instructor at the PGA training school and Vice-Captain of the PGA. A member of the *Golf World* teaching panel and a regular contributor to the magazine, he is the author of *Fit for Golf*, and co-author of the PGA teaching manual.

John Stirling's approach to hitting a golf ball is very similar to my own – simple and direct. His complete knowledge of what is required gives him the authority so essential to helping others. Coupled with this, his ever present sense of humour makes a lesson with him both rewarding and enjoyable.

I know from personal experience how difficult it is to put golf technique down on paper. I think John has done it superbly in this book, which I feel sure will be of real help to golfers of all categories.

John Jacobs

John Stirling has had tremendous experience, and I feel sure his book should help all golfers.

Gary Player

This book by John Stirling should be welcomed by golfers everywhere. John's great enthusiasm and encouragement to all his pupils can now be shared by everyone.

Tommy Horton

John Stirling has a profound knowledge of the golf swing and *every* golfer will benefit from this book.

Bernard Gallacher

Introduction

I was introduced to golf as a schoolboy during the 1939 – 1945 war. A friend told me that he could earn two shillings by carrying a golfer's bag of clubs for one round, and thus earn a substantial amount of money by doing something which he actually enjoyed. Being commercially minded, even though I was only eleven years of age, I decided to embark on a similar mission. There were several courses surrounding the village where I had been brought up, and I decided to head for the nearest one, Whitecraigs, which is about six miles south of Glasgow and one mile north of Newton Mearns, where I was born.

It was there that I started a lifelong love affair with the game. The smell of the newly mown grass, the fresh air and the lovely undulating land on which the course had been constructed, all combined so perfectly, and seemed to provide the perfect arena for this fascinating game. The actual playing of the game also appealed to me. There were such a variety of shots required, some needing the athletic co-ordination and strength of the hammer thrower, and others requiring the skill and delicate touch of a surgeon.

My first opportunity to play arrived shortly after my first caddying assignment. The Assistant Professional, who was running the golf shop as the Senior Professional was serving in the Royal Navy, asked me to help him clean the members' clubs and golf shoes. This was a service provided by most golf shops in the old days. When we had completed these duties, the Assistant would go out and practise or play a few holes, and I was invited to go along. After watching him hit shots, I naturally copied what he did, and found that I was able to hit the ball fairly consistently. Gradually, I acquired an assortment of old clubs and frequently went off to the local Municipal Golf Course. It was there that I developed an insatiable appetite for the game.

After a spell as an amateur at Eastwood, I decided in the autumn of 1951 to take the plunge, and moved south to the London area, as I had been advised that there were more openings for professionals there than in Scotland. It was some months before I finally secured a post as an Assistant Professional. This was at the Roehampton Club in South West London. After three years there, I was appointed Senior Professional at the Woking Golf Club in the heart of Surrey.

After seven years at Woking, I became Senior Professional at Meyrick Park, a municipal golf course in the centre of Bournemouth. I spent over twenty-one years there, before moving to my present position at Meon Valley Hotel Golf and Country Club in Hampshire.

During the early years at Meyrick Park I combined tournament golf with that of being a club professional. This sometimes proved difficult, and after qualifying for and playing in the Open Championship in 1966 at Muirfield, I decided to quit major tournaments and concentrate on being a club professional. One of the main duties of a club professional is that of teaching people, and I am fortunate in that I enjoy teaching. Whilst the fee one receives for a lesson is a form of reward, the real reward is in seeing the pupil improve. This does not always happen, as people find it very difficult to change their existing methods. But even those who cannot play very well can still enjoy the smell of the newly mown grass, the fresh air, and a pleasant walk in the country.

ORIGINS OF THE GAME

The earliest references to golf were made in Scotland in the middle of the fifteenth century. At that time the game was officially prohibited, as the Scottish Parliament decided that people were neglecting their archery practice by playing golf in their spare time. No doubt they felt that it would be easier to repel the English invaders with bows and arrows than golf clubs and golf balls. Although most people accept that golf originated in Scotland, there are some landscapes painted by Dutch artists before the above mentioned period, showing people playing a game on ice, using long hockey type sticks and a flat black object, which they struck with the sticks to a target. Historians tell us that this game was called Kolven and the name golf may have been derived from this. No matter who is right, it is unanimously accepted that the popular game of today originated in Scotland. In fact, as early as the reign of James II it had become a national pastime.

Links

The game was played mainly on the fine sandy turf which is found in abundance on both the east and west coasts of Scotland. It is in these areas that we now find the great championship links. In the east we have one of the Open Championship venues, Muirfield, which has, in close proximity, the three excellent Gullane courses and only a few more miles away, North Berwick. If one travels from Muirfield towards Edinburgh there are many other fine courses; Luffness, Longniddry and Musselburgh are three which should be placed on every touring golfer's itinerary. In fact Mussel-

burgh, which is inside the local racecourse, was one of the original Open Championship venues in the nineteenth century and many well-known professionals of that era came from there.

Moving northwards we come to the home of golf, St Andrews, where we find the most famous golf course in the world, the Old Course. It has been the scene of many epic battles in the game, having been the venue for many Open and Amateur Championships. St Andrews breathes golf; one has only to wander through the streets of this small university town for a short time to become aware of it. The town has several other fine courses in addition to the Old Course and they are all within walking distance of the town centre. No really keen golfer or historian of the game should go through life without visiting St Andrews.

Another famous course in the east is Carnoustie, which has been the scene of many famous championships. The town itself is very small and, like St Andrews, golf seems to be the main industry. Carnoustie was the birthplace of many of the original Scottish professionals, who emigrated to the United States towards the end of the nineteenth century.

On the west coast there are also many famous links courses, the best known being Royal Troon, Turnberry and Prestwick. The first two are modern Open Championship venues and the third was used for the same purpose until early in the twentieth century. Alas it is now considered too old-fashioned and not quite difficult enough to challenge the modern gladiators of the game. These courses are all in the county of Ayrshire, which overall must have more good golf courses than any other part of Scotland.

Moving south to England we find an area which closely rivals Ayrshire for good golf, Southport in Lancashire. Here we find the famous Royal Birkdale course, which is firmly established as a modern Open Championship venue, and other such fine courses as Hillside, Formby, and Southport and Ainsdale. Two other famous courses in England are the Royal Lytham and St Annes Golf Club on the Lancashire coast and Royal St Georges at Sandwich in Kent, both of which, with Royal Birkdale, make up the three courses in England on the Open Championship rota.

Virtually all the courses I have mentioned are described as links courses. This is because they were created in those parts of the country which link the land with the sea and in many cases are on land which thousands of years ago was under the sea. There are also many famous inland courses in the United Kingdom which are used as venues for major tournaments.

ETIQUETTE

No one should be allowed on a golf course until they have acquainted themselves with the simple rules of etiquette. It makes the game much more enjoyable, not only for the player but everyone else on the course. The rules of etiquette consist of a series of dos and don'ts and are as follows:

1. Don't move, talk, or stand directly behind the ball when a player is making a stroke.
2. Don't play until the match in front is out of range.
3. Do invite oncoming matches through if you have lost a ball in an area where it may take some time to find it.
4. Do let people whom you have invited to play through get out of range before you continue with your own game.
5. Do replace all pieces of turf removed during practice swings or when actually making the stroke. Smooth out the surface of the bunkers after playing your shot. Repair pitch-

marks made by your ball when landing on the green. Also tidy up any damage made by shoe spikes.
6. Don't take trolleys close to the edges of greens or on to the teeing areas.
7. Don't flick the ball out of the hole with the toe of your putter; this can cause damage to the edges of the hole.
8. Do leave the vicinity of the green as soon as the last player holes out. Mark scorecards on the next tee.
9. Do play at all times without undue delay.
10. Do invite oncoming matches through, if for physical reasons you have to play slowly. This makes for a more comfortable and pleasant round for everyone.

Read through these points and memorise and apply them. Other golfers will respect you for this.

WHAT IS YOUR HANDICAP?

This is one of the first questions which one is asked when trying to join a golf club. Most clubs shake their heads and say sorry to the applicant who does not have a handicap. There is a way of obtaining an official handicap. That is by going along to a municipally operated golf course, which normally has an organised club made up of the regular users of the course. These are normally run on similar lines to a private club, and if they are affiliated to the local County Golf Union can allocate handicaps.

The normal requirement is to have three cards marked by a member of the club, with the words 'for handicap' written on the card. These cards will be scrutinised by the appropriate committee and a handicap will be allocated in relation to how the player has scored against the standard scratch score of

Fig 1   Nick Faldo, one of the best European
         players. Note how his lower body and
         arms move in perfect harmony.

the course. The maximum handicap for ladies is thirty-six and for men twenty-eight.

Another way of obtaining a handicap is to join a golfing society at work. Many big firms have golfing societies. This type of handicap is not considered an official one but gives people an approximate idea of a player's playing ability.

Joining a Golf Club

Joining a golf club is not an easy matter, as most of them have full memberships nowadays. Find out if any of your friends or workmates are members of the local club and ask them what the position is regarding the possibility of becoming a member. Most clubs require an applicant to fill in an application form which asks for a reasonable amount of information about the prospective member. It also has a space for a Proposer and a Seconder, both of whom are expected to have known the applicant for some length of time. If you do not know anyone who is a member, make an appointment to see the Secretary. He normally controls the day-to-day running of the club and is able to supply the answers to most questions.

1 Equipment

A HALF-SET FOR A BEGINNER

In my opinion, the even numbered clubs are preferable for beginners. The number 1 wood, with its relatively deep face and lack of loft, is an extremely difficult club to use. Even experienced players find that their shots with this club are less reliable than those which are played with the shorter and more lofted number 3 wood. The same can be said of the irons; the numbers 2 and 3 being the most difficult to play, because of their length and lack of loft.

Ideally one should choose a number 2 and a number 4 wood, 4, 6 and 8-irons and pitching wedge or sand wedge. A light bag and a putter, and the player has all the clubs required to start playing round the course.

Seek Advice

It is advisable to go to a qualified professional for equipment, the obvious one being the person who is giving the initial lessons. He will know what type of clubs will be best suited to your build and physical strength. These are factors which must always be taken into consideration. The question of shoes and protective clothing can also be discussed with the professional. Both these items fall into various price categories as do clubs and bags. Most professionals carry fairly extensive stocks of low, medium and high cost equipment. Ask how much or how little the basic requirements will come to and buy whatever you can comfortably afford.

Always bear in mind that clubs have a trade-in value, when the player decides to move up-market. Therefore it is important to look after your clubs. Follow the advice given on the care of equipment.

PURCHASING CLUBS

Many people buy golf clubs from department stores or through mail order firms because they sometimes cost less than if they purchased them from a golf professional. This is false economy as they invariably end up with a set of clubs which are totally unsuitable for them. The four most important factors when buying clubs are:

1. To check that each club lies properly when the player assumes the correct posture at address.
2. To have the correct shaft flex.
3. To have the correct grip thickness.
4. To have a set of clubs which are accurately swingweighted and suitable for the player's physique.

Every qualified golf professional can offer advice on all of these points.

The Lie of the Club *(Fig 2)*

In order to check the lie of the club, the player should apply the correct hold on the grip of the club. The correct posture must now be assumed, by raising the arms and club together until the club is about two feet (60 cm) above the ground.

With the feet together and the legs straight

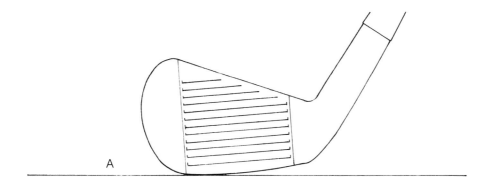

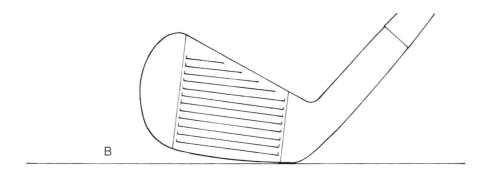

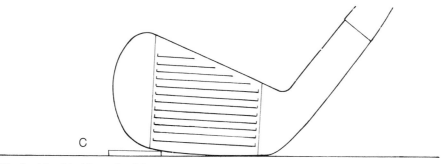

Fig 2   *The lie of the club; A lie too flat; B lie too
          upright; C ideal lie.*

the player should bend forward from the hips until the base of the club touches the ground. The feet should then be spread to the stance width appropriate to the club being used, and the knees should be slightly flexed. If the lie of the club is correct there should be a slight gap between the toe end of the base of the club and the ground, enough for a ten pence piece to be slipped underneath for about one inch. The reason for this is that the shaft bows slightly coming into impact and the gap at address allows for this.

If, when the correct posture has been assumed, there is a large gap between the toe end of the base of the club and the ground, the club's lie would be described as being too upright. A club of this type would produce shots which would travel leftwards. This is caused by the heel end of the base cutting into the turf at impact and the toe end, being above turf level, passes the heel end and closes the clubface. The reverse happens if the heel end of the club is well clear of the ground when the player has addressed the ball properly. This is described as being too flat and will produce shots which travel rightwards.

Shaft Flex

Golf shafts come in different flexes, ranging from very flexible to very stiff and they have an important bearing on the playing characteristics of a club. A strong, low handicap male golfer would hit further with ladies' flexible shafts but he would be very erratic with regard to direction. Conversely, an elderly lady using stiff shafts would hit the ball very straight but would be unable to generate any clubhead speed, which, when squarely applied, creates distance.

The four main shaft flexes fitted by manufacturers are: (L) ladies; (A) active shafts suitable for elderly men or strong ladies; (R) regular flex suitable for average men or strong, low handicap ladies; (S) stiff shafts suitable for strong, low handicap men. There is also an (X) extra stiff shaft available for very strong tournament professionals, but no club golfers would be advised to have these shafts fitted to their clubs.

Grip Thickness

The grip thickness is very important. Grips which are too thick deaden the responsive wrist action on both the backward and forward swings. Thin grips on the other hand will create a very loose wristed type of action. Apart from the fact that grips which are not the correct thickness affect the actual swing, the feeling of discomfort at the address damages the player's confidence.

Swingweight

Swingweighting of clubs is a fairly modern method of producing a set of clubs in which every club in the set feels the same when the player swings it. The swingweight is related to the shaft flex, and a shaft flex for ladies (L) will be fitted to a club about C6 to C8, a shaft flex (R) for men will be about C9 to D2 and a shaft flex (S) D3 to D6. Most professionals' shops have a swingweight machine, so the prospective buyer can have the clubs accurately checked.

Beware of clubs that are too heavy, they reduce clubhead speed and tend to make the player feel tired towards the end of a round. Clubs that are too light, particularly in the clubheads, can also have a detrimental effect on a player's performance.

A qualified professional will be able to provide sound advice on choosing clubs, and of course will be delighted to teach you how to use them.

Irons	Loft factor	Distance
2-iron	18°	approx. 190 yards (174 metres)
3-iron	22°	approx. 180 yards (165 metres)
4-iron	26°	approx. 170 yards (155 metres)
5-iron	30°	approx. 160 yards (146 metres)
6-iron	34°	approx. 150 yards (137 metres)
7-iron	38°	approx. 140 yards (128 metres)
8-iron	42°	approx. 130 yards (119 metres)
9-iron	46°	approx. 120 yards (110 metres)
Pitching wedge	52°	approx. 100 yards (91 metres)
Sand-iron	58°	approx. 80 yards (73 metres)

Woods	Loft factor	Distance
No. 1 wood	12°	approx. 245 yards (224 metres)
No. 2 wood	16°	approx. 235 yards (215 metres)
No. 3 wood	20°	approx. 225 yards (206 metres)
No. 4 wood	24°	approx. 215 yards (197 metres)
No. 5 wood	28°	approx. 205 yards (187 metres)

Loft and Shaft Length

The loft of a golf club is the number of degrees at which the face of the club is set back from a vertical line.

In a matched set of irons, the low numbered clubs have the least amount of loft and the longest shafts, and the high numbered clubs have the greatest amount of loft and the shortest shafts. Thus, the long shafted, low numbered clubs are the weapons for long low shots, whereas the short shafted, high numbered clubs are used for the short high shots.

There are four degrees of loft between each club, starting with eighteen degrees of loft on a 2-iron, and progressing through to a 9-iron with forty-six degrees of loft.

As the clubs go up in number, so the shafts are shortened by half an inch per club. This shortening process, plus the increasing loft, makes the ball travel a shorter distance, by approximately ten to twelve yards for each club.

The distances a male low handicap player would be expected to hit the ball are as above. These distances are inevitably approximate, based on a typical player in reasonable conditions. Each player should find his or her personal distance in practice.

This is done by using a 6-iron and twelve reasonable practice balls. Hit the balls on a flat piece of ground on a calm day, and count the number of walking paces from where you hit the balls to the middle of the group. The number of paces should be noted, and as the average pace represents one yard, you will know how far, on average, you hit the 6-iron. It is then an easy matter to add or subtract a number of yards to find the distance which can be obtained with the other clubs in the set.

Obviously, not everyone will be able to take a pace which approximates one yard. This problem can be solved by measuring twenty-five yards with a tape measure. Find out how many of your own paces are required to cover this distance, and multiply this number by four to find out how many paces are required to cover one hundred yards.

Many of the fit young tournament players hit the ball much greater distances than those outlined above. This is due to such factors as better technique, strength, and daily practice. They also tend to use less lofted clubs than amateurs, not because they want to hit the ball further, but mainly to send it through the air with a lower trajectory. Whereas the average player may have difficulty getting the ball airborne, the professional has problems keeping it down.

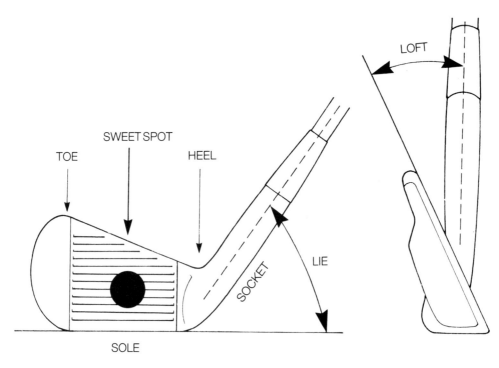

TOE   SWEET SPOT   HEEL   LOFT   SOCKET   LIE   SOLE

Fig 3   *Lie and loft.*

CHOICE OF BALL

I am often asked by customers in my golf shop which ball I suggest they should play with. I can normally supply the answer right away if it is one of my own club members, whose standard of golf is familiar to me, but if it is somebody visiting the course then I have to know something about their level of ability before advising them. Naturally I am generally biased towards the ball which I choose to play with, because I like its playing characteristics. The important characteristics are the compression, the durability and feel at impact. Everyone should look for the above qualities in a ball.

Size

In recent years golfers in Britain have accepted that the American size ball is better than the slightly smaller British size ball, which is 1.62in against its American counterpart at 1.68in. The larger ball sits up better on the fairways, is easier to chip and pitch with and holds its line better on the greens. The smaller ball is still legal in this country except in major competitions but I feel that it will disappear altogether from the golfing scene in the very near future.

Type

Most manufacturers make balls of different types. Some have solid centres covered by a cut-resistant cover, made from man-made materials, whilst others are made up of tightly wound elastic, covered by a material called balata.

The first type are much more durable but

10

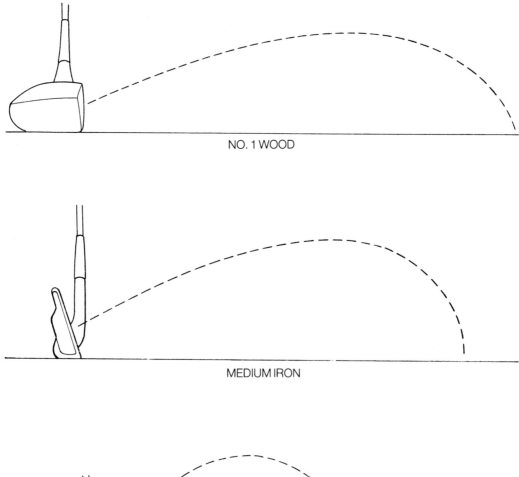

NO. 1 WOOD

MEDIUM IRON

SHORT IRON

Fig 4   *How the club's loft affects the trajectory of the ball.*

tend to feel hard and are inclined to be a bit lively when they land, thus making short game control more difficult. The second type are the choice of the good player, who puts feel and control before durability. There is not a great deal to choose between the two different types as far as distance is concerned. If anything, the solid centre ball might travel a little further because of its liveliness on landing, but this gain in distance is generally offset by the control gained with the other type of ball around the green.

Compression

The compression of a ball can also affect its performance. Most of the solid balls have a compression factor of between ninety and one hundred, which is considered fairly high and means that they will not flatten very much at impact. Conventionally wound balls are available in eighty, ninety and one hundred compression. Eighty, being the easiest to flatten, is ideal for ladies and short hitting men, ninety is ideal for strong ladies and medium hitting men and the one hundred compression ball is best for top class amateurs and professionals.

In cold weather it is wise to use a slightly lower compression than normal, and it also improves the performance of a ball if it has been in a fairly warm room prior to being used.

Whichever type of ball you choose, stick to it and get accustomed to the feel of it. This is very important, particularly with short shots.

CARE OF EQUIPMENT

Many golfers fail to take care of their equipment. This is not only expensive in the long run, but makes them play less efficiently. Starting with clubs, it is amazing how few players ever wash their rubber grips. If this is done after every four or five rounds, the grips will come up like new. Just add a little detergent to some fairly hot water, give each grip a firm scrub with a brush and rinse off. The heads should also be kept clean, as grass and mud quickly fill the lines on the clubfaces. This makes it impossible to obtain any backspin on one's shots.

Always remove head covers from the woods after playing in the rain. Wet covers left for any length of time on these clubs will cause swelling of the blocks.

Shoes are also very important, and should be cleaned off after each round. If the underfoot conditions are wet, make sure that leather shoes are dried slowly in a reasonably warm temperature. Always use shoe trees or, if none are available, fill the shoes with rolled up newspaper.

Waterproof clothing should always be hung out after playing in the rain. Crumpling it up and throwing it into the clothing pocket of the golf bag will soon rot the material of the clothing and the bag. The same applies to the golf umbrella; open it up and let it dry in a reasonably warm atmosphere.

2 The Swing

ADDRESSING THE BALL

Addressing the ball correctly is as important as aiming a rifle and getting comfortably set before pulling the trigger. In golf, the procedure is very similar to rifle shooting, in that there is a target and the objective is to hit the target or get as near as possible to it with every shot.

The five main factors in addressing the ball are; aim, hold, ball position, stance and alignment, and posture. To ensure a correct set-up read the following over and over again and then practise it repeatedly until it becomes automatic.

Note – the following instructions are for right-handed players. If you are left-handed, for right read left and vice versa.

Aim *(Fig 5)*

Stand about two yards (or metres) behind the ball and draw an imaginary line from the target back to the ball and pick a spot on the ground three to five feet (0.9–1.5 m) in front of the ball. Keeping this spot clearly in one's mind, lay all of the sole of the club on the ground and at the same time set the bottom front edge at right angles to the ball-to-spot line.

It is very important that the sole of the club is placed correctly as this leaves the maker's loft on the club exactly as intended. This will also position the top of the grip correctly, which will assist the player in arriving at the correct ball position and also the body position. The top of the grip should be opposite the inside of the left thigh, when assuming a correct stance. It should also be level with the ball.

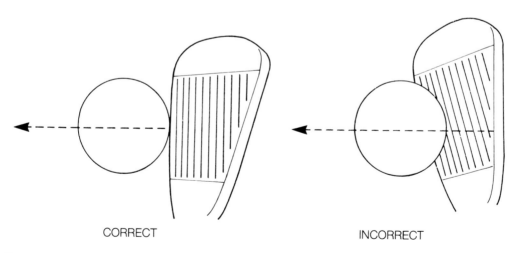

CORRECT   INCORRECT

Fig 5   *Lining the sole of the club square with the ball-to-target line.*

The Swing

Hold *(Figs 6 to 8)*

Most teachers use the word grip when describing the application of the hands to the club; I prefer the word hold, as grip implies tightness, which in fact is the last thing one wants when holding a golf club in preparation for the swing. Hold the club firmly enough to control it but lightly enough to be aware of the head of it.

The positioning of the hands is vital and most of the shots which swerve to the right or left can be attributed to an incorrect hold.

The left hand should be placed on the club first and it is advisable to leave about three quarters of an inch (19 mm) of the club protruding from the butt end of the hand. This helps the player to control the club more

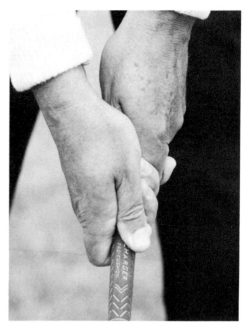

Fig 6   *An orthodox hold. Two to three knuckles visible on the left hand, and the vees pointing between the chin and the right shoulder.*

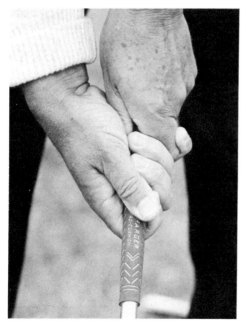

Fig 7   *A typical hooker's hold. Four knuckles visible on the left hand, and the vees pointing outside the right shoulder.*

Fig 8   *A typical slicer's hold. Hardly showing the first knuckle on the left hand, and the vees pointing to the left shoulder.*

effectively. Hang the left arm in a comfortably straight position by the side of the body with the back of the hand facing the target, and then move the hand out in front of the body until the butt end of the hand is four or five inches (10–12.5 cm) from the inside of the left thigh. The grip of the club should then be laid diagonally across the hand starting from the middle joint of the forefinger to approximately one inch (25 mm) below the base of the little finger. The fingers should now be curled round the grip with a sensation of a gentle amount of pressure being applied by the little finger and the two fingers next to it.

The right arm should then be placed to the right side of the body with the palm of the hand flat against the side of the thigh. From this position, swing the arm out and bring the palm squarely against the shaft, just below the left hand. The club should be held in the fingers of the right hand. This does not feel as strong and secure as holding it in the palm would.

It is advisable to get used to holding it in the fingers right from the start, as it will soon become natural and comfortable.

Different Methods

The three main methods of holding the club are:

1. The Vardon or overlapping hold.
2. The interlocking hold.
3. The double-handed hold.

The Vardon is the most popular method, and is arrived at by placing the little finger of the right hand over the forefinger of the left hand, or in the cleft between the forefinger and the finger next to it. The interlocking hold is also popular and many top tournament players throughout the world use it. In this hold the little finger of the right hand and the forefinger of the left hand intertwine. In the third method all of the fingers of both hands are placed on the grip of the club.

When the hold is finally arrived at, the left thumb should be slightly to the right of the centre of the shaft and the right thumb slightly to the left. This enables both thumbs to form small vees with the base of each forefinger. Those vees should point between the chin and the right shoulder. This is described as an orthodox or neutral position. If they pointed straight up to the chin it would be known as a slicer's hold, and conversely if they pointed to the right of the shoulder it would be known as a hooker's hold.

In order to familiarise oneself with the feel of the correct hold and also to strengthen the hands and wrists, it is a good idea to have a short heavy club, such as a sand-iron, at home and to place the hands on the grip in the proper hold position and waggle the wrists and clubhead from side to side at a fairly vigorous pace. Initially, the hands and wrists will tire quickly, but by doing the exercise frequently the strength and condition of both will gradually improve.

Ball Position

Many top tournament players advocate that the ball should be played from a point opposite the inside of the left heel for all shots. The narrowing of the stance brings the right foot closer to the ball as the clubs become shorter rather than the ball being moved back towards the right foot. This system works very well for players of this calibre, but the average player will fare better by adopting the system whereby the ball is opposite the left heel for wood shots from the tee and all long shots through to the 4-iron, providing the ball is lying well. With the medium irons, numbers 5, 6 and 7 it should be positioned about two inches (5 cm) to the right of the heel. For short irons it should be placed in the centre of the

The Swing

narrowest stance.

The method of varying the ball position in order to play special shots will be dealt with in the appropriate sections later in the book.

Stance and Alignment *(Fig 9)*

Many people playing golf are under the impression that lines drawn across the toes and

Fig 9 *The shoulders, hips, and knees should be parallel to the ball-to-target line, as if on railway lines.*

shoulders should point directly at the target; this is not so. They should be parallel to the ball-to-target line. Think of railway lines; the clubhead, ball and target on one, and the player's shoulder line and feet line on the other.

The procedure for adopting the correct stance and shoulder alignment, after having ensured that the bottom edge of the clubface has been set accurately and the club is being held properly, is for the player to measure off the correct distance at which to stand from

Fig 10   *The first stage in learning to assume the correct posture. Stand perfectly erect with the legs straight.*

the ball. This is achieved by adding the left arm to the shaft as the upper section of the measuring instrument. The arm should be comfortably straight and hanging in front of the body, with the top of the shaft about four or five inches (10–12.5 cm) clear of the inside of the left thigh. Do not raise the wrists or drop them into unnatural positions. They should be in exactly the same situation as when the arms are hanging comfortably straight by the sides of the body. Using the correctly aimed bottom edge of the clubface as the reference point, set the shoulders and the line across the toes at right angles to it. This creates the parallelism which assists the player in swinging the clubhead true to the correct plane.

Fig 11 *Stage two: bend forward from the hips until the base of the club is lying correctly on the ground.*

Posture *(Figs 10 to 12)*

In order to swing the club in a smooth co-ordinated manner it is essential to adopt the correct posture at address. This can be practised by raising the arms and club together until the head of the club is about two feet (60 cm) from the ground. The player should now bend forward from the hip joints until the base of the club is almost flat on the ground. The amount of body bending required varies slightly according to the length of the club being used. It is this variation that creates the different planes on which the different length clubs should be swung. With the spinal angle correctly set the player should now flex both knees. This should create a feeling of being poised and ready to move smoothly in unison with the swinging arms and club.

Fig 12 *Stage three: flex the knees forwards and inwards. Practise this method of arriving at the correct posture with various clubs.*

THE BACKSWING

(Figs 13 to 16)

Most players have a slight forward press prior to starting the club on its journey away from the ball. In some cases, for example Gary Player, this forward press movement is very distinctive, and in others it is almost imperceptible. It usually consists of a slight leftward movement of the inside of the right knee, which is accompanied by a slight turn of the hips to the left. The actual movement of the clubhead and hands starts in unison with the hips and right knee as they return to their original positions.

At the beginning of the backswing, the clubhead, hands and arms must move as one unit. This one-piece movement will trigger off a responsive turning movement in the shoulders which will cause the clubhead to curve gradually inwards as it swings back. The player should feel that the clubface remains at right angles to the arc of the swing and not to the ball-to-target line. The shoulders and hips turn at right angles to the tilted spine, which is a variable factor as we play different length clubs. For instance, when we are playing a number 1 wood shot, we do not bend over at the hips as much as we would with a 9-iron with its shorter shaft.

It is vital that the spine's address angle is maintained throughout the swing and this, plus the comfortably straight left arm, will enable the clubhead to arc around the body at the correct angle with a constant radius. The player should visualise a wheel tilted at the

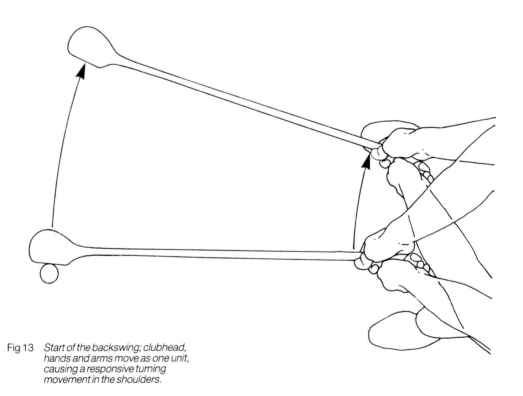

Fig 13 *Start of the backswing; clubhead, hands and arms move as one unit, causing a responsive turning movement in the shoulders.*

Fig 14 *Jerry Pate, former US Open Champion. Here he illustrates how the arms and shoulders work in unison with the swinging club.*

The Swing

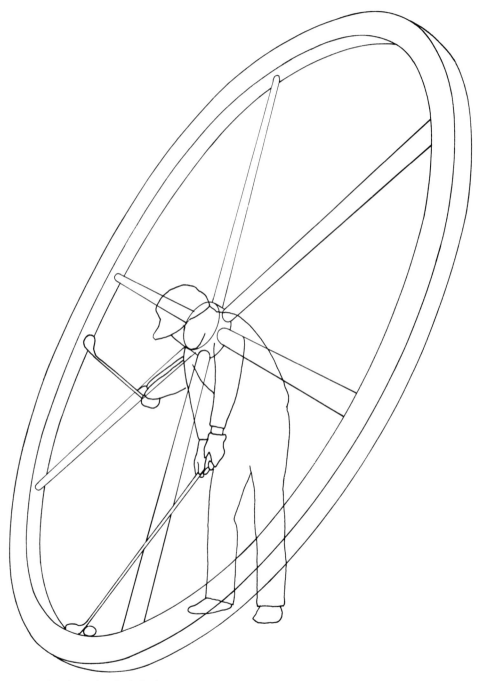

Fig 15   *Visualise the neck as the hub of a
         wheel, and move the clubhead back
         up and around the rim.*

neck-to-ball angle, of which the neck is the hub, and endeavour to move the clubhead back and up around the rim. At the top of the backswing, the player should have turned the shoulders through ninety degrees, the hips through forty-five degrees, and the left knee should have moved inwards to point four or five inches (10–12.5 cm) to the right of the ball.

The other important points to strive for are to ensure that the left thumb and right wrist are under the shaft and that the shaft is parallel to the ball-to-target line. The wrists arrive in this cocked position as a result of the club swinging backwards, and about halfway through the backswing it moves up and over the right shoulder in conjunction with the turning shoulders.

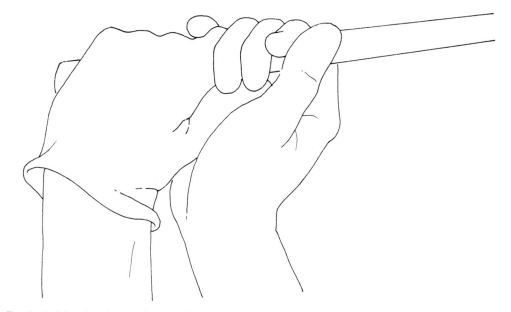

Fig 16   *Left thumb and right wrist should be under the shaft at the top of the backswing.*

Fig 17   *(overleaf) Jack Nicklaus, probably the world's greatest player, just starting the downswing. The knees are about to begin their leftward thrust.*

Fig 18   *(page 25) Eamonn D'Arcy, the Irish Ryder Cup player, proving that you do not have to be orthodox to be a top class player. Note how the fleshy pad of the right thumb has come away from the left thumb. The left arm is also a little too bent.*

Checkpoints

The main points in achieving a consistently successful backswing are as follows:

1. A smooth one-piece movement of the clubhead, hands and arms.
2. The trunk turn beginning to respond to the above swinging action.
3. Allow the clubhead to curve gradually inwards and upwards around the rim of the imaginary wheel.
4. Feel that the shoulders, hips and left knee are winding up in unison with the swinging clubhead, hands and arms.
5. At the completion of the backswing make sure that the shoulders have turned through ninety degrees, the hips forty-five, and that the left knee is pointing to a spot four or five inches (10–12.5 cm) to the right of the ball.
6. The wrists should be cocked so that they set the club parallel to the ball-to-target line, left thumb and right wrist under the shaft.
7. Remember to maintain a constant spinal angle and a comfortably straight left arm throughout the backswing.

THE DOWNSWING
(Figs 19 to 21)

The downswing actually starts just before the completion of the backswing. Slow motion films of all the best players show that the left knee starts to move to the left just as the hands are arriving at the end of their backward journey. The action in the knee is very soon accompanied by the reverse action of the hands and arms. This is felt as a downwards pulling action with the last three fingers of the left hand. This action fully cocks the wrists in readiness for the fast unleashing hand movement required to square the clubface at impact.

Many people have written about late hitting being the answer to successful golf. They usually substantiate their theory by showing photographs of leading players with their hands almost opposite the ball and the wrists still fully cocked. Beware of trying to emulate this position unless you are trying to produce a violent slice. Try to hit on time, rather than late, is my advice. Visualise the clubhead being applied freely and squarely into the back of the ball. Feel that it is slinging the ball in the direction of the target and that the lower body movement, which was initiated by the sideways action of the left knee, develops into a turning movement of the hips and shoulders. This turning or unwinding body movement must be synchronised to the swinging arms and clubhead.

Too much emphasis on the body unwinding tends to leave the clubhead behind the

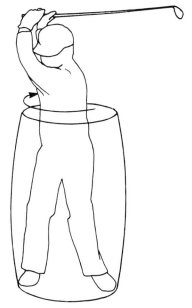

Fig 19   *Turn the body to the right as though standing inside a barrel.*

Fig 20   Tom Watson, currently one of the
world's best players, approaching
impact. Note that his right arm is still
bent, waiting to deliver the blow as the
club meets the ball.

hands at impact. By the same token, too much emphasis on clubhead and hands will tend to make the clubhead pass the hands before impact. The first fault would cause the ball to set off rightwards immediately after impact and the second fault would produce the opposite effect.

After the clubhead has been swung freely through the ball in the direction of the target, it should swing inwards and upwards. This will carry the clubhead up and over the left shoulder to finish up pointing to the ground with the clubshaft diagonally across the back. At this point in the swing, make sure that the centre of the body, and head and eyes have turned to face the target. Ensure also that the body weight has flowed through on to the outside edge of the left shoe and that all of the sole of the right shoe is looking directly away from the target.

Checkpoints

The main points to remember are as follows:

1. Feel the left knee and the left hand pulling leftwards to start the downswing.
2. Uncock the wrists so that the clubhead arrives at the ball on time.
3. Synchronise arm swing and body unwinding.
4. Make the clubhead travel up and around the rim of the imaginary wheel after impact.
5. Finish in a fully unwound balanced position.

Fig 21 *(opposite) Hale Irwin, winner of two US Opens, just arriving at impact. Compare his right arm with Tom Watson's and see how much it straightens in that small segment of the swing.*

PLANE AND ARC

The plane of the golf swing is the angle of the clubhead's path or arc in relation to the ground. If the clubhead travelled straight back from the ball and continued on that line it would describe an arc which would be at a ninety degree angle to the ground. This would be much too upright and in fact would create a situation where the clubshaft would finish the backward journey in front of the player's eyes. Conversely, if the clubhead never left the ground and described a circle around the body, this would be much too flat. Ideally, the correct plane will be somewhere between these two extremes.

The plane is controlled by the posture, the angle of the spine and the hang of the arms being the determining factors. For instance, when a player has to play a ball which is above the feet, the spine is more vertical and the arms are more horizontal than on a normal shot. This would automatically produce a flat plane. The reverse applies when the ball is below the feet. Here the spine is bent forward more than usual and the arms hang downwards, thus producing an upright plane.

Players who are prone to swinging too flat or too upright can actually derive a great deal of benefit from practising with the ball above or below their feet according to their particular malady.

When the ball is level with the feet we also have variations in the angle of the plane. With the short irons the spine tilts further forward and the feet are closer to the ball, thereby producing a more upright plane. The longer shafted woods, with the player's spine nearer to the vertical and the feet further from the ball, produce a flatter plane. Ideally, the swing plane should be parallel to a line drawn from the centre of the lowest part of the neck to the ball.

Width of Arc

This is an expression which frequently crops up when professionals or top class amateurs are discussing the golf swing. Arc width is the measurement between the left shoulder and the left hand, and is maintained by keeping the left arm comfortably straight throughout the backswing and downswing until the left elbow folds halfway through the follow-through stage of the swing. This folding should be allowed to happen naturally, otherwise the player will tend to push most of the shots to the right of the target. When we add the shaft length of the particular club being used to the player's arms, we have the radius of the arc.

Obviously the shaft cannot bend, so by making sure that the arm remains comfortably straight through the segment of the swing described above, we will maintain a constant radius. Visualising the arm and shaft as the spoke of a wheel tilted on the neck-to-ball line will help the player to establish a grooved swing. Try to make the head of the club travel back and up around the rim of the imaginary wheel and return it to the ball along the same path as it enters the hitting area. Photographs and films have shown us that the clubhead actually drops underneath the rim as it changes from the backswing to forward swing. This is caused by the lateral movement of the knees and the completion of the wrist cock. Do not be too concerned with this, just concentrate on tracking the clubhead away from the ball correctly and returning it along this path as it approaches the ball prior to impact.

Swing Sequence *(Figs 22 to 26)*

(Fig 22) An orthodox set-up. Hands opposite the inside of the left thigh, feet and shoulders parallel to the ball-to-target line. No tension in legs, hands or arms.

(Fig 23) Halfway back, with the arms making
the swing, and the left shoulder, hip and knee
responding.

(Fig 24) At the top of the backswing, with the left shoulder and knee in the same vertical plane. Left thumb and right wrist underneath the shaft, and left heel slightly off the ground.

(Fig 25) Halfway through after impact. Hands
and clubface are square to the shoulders;
right shoulder, hip and knee responding to the
swinging club and arms.

(Fig 26) The completion of the follow-through. Body facing the target, with the weight fully through onto the left leg. Note position of head and eyes, and the right heel.

3 Shot Making

Players should note that all instructions in this chapter relate to right-handed players. If you are left-handed, the instructions should be 'handed'; i.e. for right read left and vice versa.

PUTTING *(Figs 27 to 31)*

Putting is often regarded as the least exciting part of the game. The fact that very little physical strength or movement is required, conveys the impression that virtually anyone should be able to putt reasonably well. This concept is reinforced by the fact that thousands of people on holiday hire a putter and a ball and proceed to cope fairly effectively on the municipal putting green.

To the tournament player, however, putting is the most exciting and rewarding part of the game. Anyone who is not a better than average putter finds it extremely difficult to make any sort of living from tournament golf. Statistics show that an average of around thirty putts per round is required if one hopes to be highly successful. That average has to be achieved on greens where the holes are usually cut in the most difficult places, especially in the last round of a tournament.

In the past, there have been all sorts of putting methods, and even some of the most unorthodox have been extremely effective. But the modern tournament players have evolved a more standardised system. This system has eliminated as many moving parts as possible, and it is the one which I recommend to anyone who is starting golf, or anyone who is putting badly with their existing method.

Technique

Putting is like any other stroke, in that it requires a correct address position before actually making the stroke. The aim is taken in the same way as any other shot; look at the line from behind the ball and pick a spot on the ball-to-hole line. Set the clubface behind the ball with the face at right angles to this spot, and have all of the sole of the putter on the ground.

Hold comes next, and whilst there seems to be a greater variety of methods employed in holding the putter than with any other club, the most popular one amongst the world's best players is the reverse overlap. This means that the forefinger of the left hand overlaps the little finger of the right hand, the exact reverse of the overlapping hold used for all other shots. There is a feeling of more control with the right hand when using this hold, and this is an essential feeling to have when trying to roll a ball along a line to a specific point.

A narrow stance with the distance between the heels in the region of ten to twelve inches (25–30 cm) is what most good putters seem to employ. The alignment of the shoulders, hips, knees and feet should be parallel to the ball-to-target line – the railway lines principle again.

Posture is just as important in putting as it is in all other shots. The knees should be flexed forwards and inwards, and the body should be bent over until the eyeline is directly over the ball-to-target line. The player's bottom should protrude slightly to counterbalance the forward bending of the body and the knee flexion. Ideally, the player should feel that a balanced stillness can be maintained in the body as the arms and putter make the stroke.

Ball position is also critical, as the ideal point of contact is when the putter is travelling at the lowest point of its swinging arc. At this stage, it is square and travelling through to the target. Remember the impact requirements on full shots; square clubface, club path ball-to-target, correct angle of approach. The successful putt requires the first two, the third does not apply in putting as the club travels backwards and forwards only. Placing the back of the ball at a point opposite the inside of the left heel gives the best opportunity of achieving these correct impact factors.

The actual swing of the putter is made by the arms with the hands serving as the connecting link. Because of the forward bending at address, the arms bend slightly and it is vitally important to maintain this degree of bend throughout the stroke. Another very important feeling is that of moving the top of the shaft and the putter head back and through together. This cancels out wrist action, which can prove to be very unreliable under pressure.

Checkpoints

1. Check ball-to-target line from behind the ball and pick up a spot over which to putt.
2. Square the putter face to this spot.
3. Narrow stance and parallel alignment of shoulders, hips, knees and feet.
4. Bend forward until eyes are directly over the line. Flex knees forwards and inwards.
5. Position ball so that line across back of ball runs past the inside of the left heel.
6. Smooth back and through pendulum swing, maintaining original arm bend throughout.

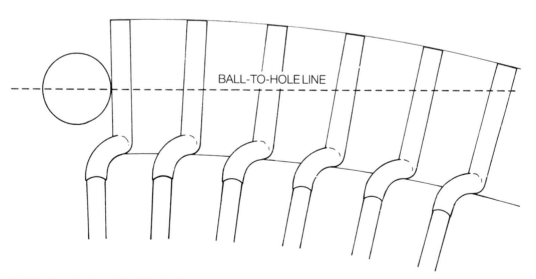

BALL-TO-HOLE LINE

Fig 27   The putter head should arc back slightly to the inside on the longer putts.

Shot Making

Fig 28   *Front view of the putting stance. Hands in line with clubhead, and both elbows bent and close to the sides of the body. A comfortable relaxed position.*

Fig 29   *A down-the-line view of a thirty foot putt with about two feet of right to left borrow. Note how the putter face is aimed to the right of the flag, and the line across the toes parallel to the ball-to-target line.*

Fig 30 *The end of the backswing for a thirty foot putt. The forearms, hands and putter are swinging in unison. No conscious wrist action.*

Fig 31 *Note how the length of the follow-through matches the length of the backswing, and how the amount of bend in the left arm has remained constant from start to fininsh.*

BUNKER SHOTS

(Figs 32 to 36)

The bunker shot encountered most frequently is the one from a greenside bunker. These bunkers seem to have a magnetic attraction for the ball, particularly in the case of players who have a fear of bunker shots. However, to a professional or a first-class amateur, the bunker shot from a reasonable lie holds no terrors. As in all other shots in golf, a sound technique is essential and I will describe what must be done to develop this.

Technique

Firstly, a good sand-iron is necessary. The pitching wedge or 9-iron will work in certain situations and are sometimes preferable when the sand is wet or hard packed, but for the majority of greenside bunker shots the sand-iron is the most suitable club. Its wide, rounded sole, with the back edge of the flange lower than the front edge, enables the clubhead to glide through the sand.

The player should open the face of the club slightly before taking a normal hold. Body alignment and stance should also be open, as this will automatically create the required steep out-to-in swing. Select a strike point about two inches (5 cm) behind the ball, and wriggle the feet into the sand to establish a firm foothold; this helps to get an awareness of the depth and texture of the sand.

The backswing should be smooth, with the wrists cocking backwards and upwards earlier than in a normal swing. On the downswing, the club should be pulled down through the ball with the left knee and left arm working in unison.

Keep your head very steady during the shot, and look keenly at the intended strike point. Make sure that the clubhead is accelerating smoothly through impact, and that the divot of sand with which the ball is thrown onto the green is not too deep.

In order to become a really first-class bunker player, a great deal of practice is required, but the less ambitious players will cope very adequately if they learn and apply the foregoing technique.

If the ball is buried or in a footprint in the bunker, a different technique is required. In this situation, the face of the club should be slightly closed. This assists in digging more deeply into the sand on impact. The ball should be placed opposite the centre of the stance which, for this shot, should be parallel. The wrists should cock early to ensure that the downswing will have the required steepness. Look at and strike a spot about one inch (25 mm) behind the ball. Strike firmly and do not expect to follow through, as the clubhead will tend to bury itself in the sand after impact. There is no backspin on a shot of this nature, so allow for run.

Summary

Normal Lie

1. Always use a sand-iron unless the sand is very wet or hard packed; in these situations use a 9-iron or pitching wedge.
2. Wriggle your feet into the sand to check its depth and texture.
3. Have sixty per cent of your weight on the left foot, and play the ball from a point opposite the left heel.
4. Set clubface slightly open at address and maintain this openness through impact.
5. Open the stance and body alignment; this assists in achieving the required steepness.
6. Look at and strike a point approximately one and a half to two inches (4–5 cm) behind the ball.
7. Throw a thin six-inch (15 cm) segment of sand in the direction of the target.

Fig 32 Note how feet and shoulders are parallel to the left-hand club on the ground. This open set-up creates the out-to-in swing required for greenside bunker shots. Note also that the clubhead is held above the sand at address, as required by the Rules of Golf.

Fig 33   *The automatic result of an open set-
up, with the shaft pointing well left of
the flag.*

8. Don't slow up on contact with the sand; always accelerate smoothly through to a good finish.

Buried Lie

1. Close clubface slightly; this creates a deeper digging action.
2. Play the ball from opposite the centre of the stance.
3. Stand with feet and shoulders parallel to ball-to-target line.
4. Look at and strike a point approximately one inch (25 mm) behind the ball.
5. Break wrists early on backswing and drive the clubhead down strongly on to the selected strike point.
6. Allow for run on this shot.
7. Do not attempt to follow through, as the clubhead tends to bury itself in the sand after impact.

Fairway Bunkers

1. Before selecting your club, always check the lie of the ball and ascertain the height required to clear the bunker face with something to spare.
2. Wriggle your feet firmly into the sand and shorten the hold on the club by the same amount as the feet go down.
3. Play the ball from the centre of the stance and look at the centre of the right-hand side of the ball.
4. Swing mainly with the arms and do not rush. Watch the ball closely and swing smoothly.

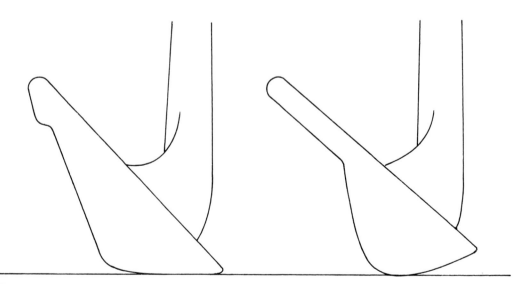

Fig 34   Pitching wedge, with the front and back edges level, and sand wedge, with its back edge lower. This is called the bounce factor.

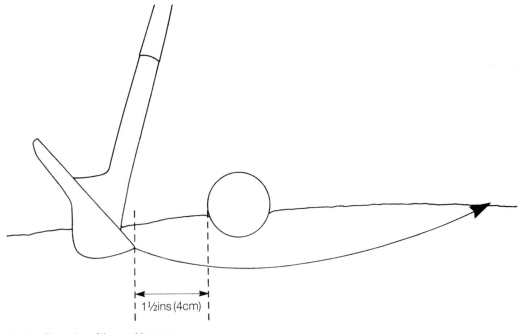

Fig 35   *The action of the sand-iron on a greenside bunker shot.*

1½ins (4cm)

SHORT IRONS *(Figs 37 to 40)*

The short irons, numbers 8, 9, wedge and sand-iron, are the clubs with which we expect to create birdie opportunities. Their shorter shafts and lofted faces make the actual striking of the ball less difficult than with the longer-shafted clubs. In order to develop the pin-point accuracy of the best players, the average golfer must develop a sound technique and practice a great deal, particularly with the pitching wedge.

Technique

The fact that the shafts are shorter means that we stand closer to the ball and this, with a gradually narrowing stance, creates a narrower and more upright swing. As already explained in the chapter discussing the arc of the golf swing, the head of the club will be travelling back and up, down and through, on a line closer to the vertical than it does with the longer-shafted clubs.

Stance

When playing these clubs, the player should adopt a narrow open stance; this assists in the smooth turning through movement of the lower body which should accompany the swinging arms and clubhead as they accelerate down and through the ball and up into a nicely balanced finish. Although an open stance is recommended, it is advisable to keep the upper body parallel to the ball-to-target line. This will assist the player in making a correct backswing arc with the clubhead.

Never underclub with short irons; this leads to off-line shots. Find out on the practice ground how far each club hits the ball when using a balanced and controlled swing.

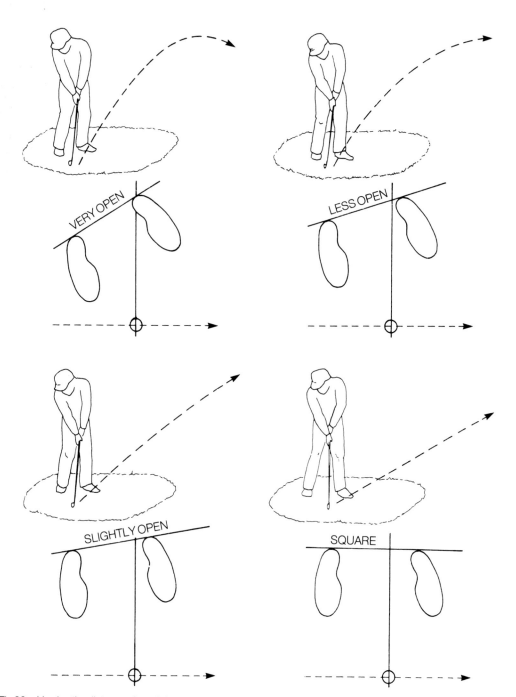

Fig 36 *Varying the distance of sand shots.*

45

Shot Making

Fig 37   *Top of the backswing with the 8-iron.
Wrists fully cocked and the shaft again
parallel to the ball-to-target line.*

Fig 38   *Just after impact with the 8-iron.*

Fig 39   *Halfway through with the 8-iron. The shaft is obscured by the body, but it can be seen that the club swings back inwards after travelling straight through impact.*

Fig 40   *The finish of the 8-iron shot. Body balanced with weight completely through on the left foot.*

Pitching *(Figs 41 to 49)*

The short irons can be used for pitching the ball close to the hole with backspin or pitch and run shots where there is plenty of green to work with. Of the two shots, the pitch and run is the easier shot to play and is generally more effective. It is easier to judge roll than flight, particularly when playing fairly short shots to undulating greens. However, there are many occasions when the player has to play the high flying pitch with stop.

The technique used to play this shot differs from the pitch and run, in that the wrists are cocked soon after the clubhead starts its backward journey from the ball. This early cocking of the wrists creates a steep narrow backswing. From this position, the player should feel that the left arm is pulling the club down towards the ball with the wrists still fully cocked. The feeling of pulling the club through the ball at impact will enable the sole of the pitching wedge or sand wedge to slide between the base of the ball and the piece of turf on which the ball is resting. It is this type of impact which creates maximum backspin on the ball, as it is being struck at the base of its vertical axis.

This shot should be practised extensively with the pitching wedge and the sand wedge, the choice of club being governed by how the ball is lying. The sand wedge should only be used if the ball is lying well, as its lower back edge tends to make the club bounce at impact and, on hard ground, this could produce a half-topped shot which would race across the green and off the other side.

(Fig 41) A comfortable address position for a short high pitch with a sand-iron. Ball opposite the centre of a narrow stance, and the hands set slightly ahead of the clubface.

(Fig 42) The end of the backswing for the short high pitch. Note the cocked wrists and the position of the clubface.

(Fig 43) Just after impact, with the ball starting to climb upwards off the face of the squarely-applied sand-iron.

(Fig 44) The completion of the short high pitch.
Note how the right hand has not rolled the
face anti-clockwise as it would on a shot
played with full power.

Wedge Pitch Sequence
(Figs 45 to 47)

(Fig 45) Note the shortened grip, and how close the hands are to the legs. The body weight is two-thirds on the left foot.

(Fig 46) Wrists cocked early to get the clubhead back and up in order to attack the ball
with a steeper blow than when playing a chip
and run.

(Fig 47) See the height of the ball, and how the head of the club has followed out towards the flag.

Fig 48   *A three quarter length backswing for a sixty yard pitch. Note the closeness of the right elbow to the side, and the fully cocked wrists.*

Fig 49   *Just after impact with the sixty yard pitch. Note how knees have moved laterally as arms have swung the club down and through impact.*

Chipping *(Figs 50 & 51)*

Another shot which every player should have in their repertoire of short strokes is the running chip. This can be played with anything between a 5-iron and a 9-iron. This shot is relatively easy to play, and should be used around the green when there are no obstacles such as bunkers, grass mounds or streams between the ball and the hole. The club selection should be based on how much fairway has to be carried before reaching the green, and how much green there is for the ball to roll along before reaching the hole. A small amount of fairway to be carried and a large amount of green to roll along, would call for a shot with a 5 or 6-iron, and if the situation was reversed the 8 or 9-iron should be used.

Stance

The stance required for these chip and run shots should be narrow, with the left foot withdrawn about two inches (5 cm). This opening of the stance enables the player to obtain a better ball-to-target perspective. This is essential when playing these short shots which call for pin-point accuracy. The body weight should be distributed with two thirds of the weight on the left foot at address. This should be maintained throughout the playing of the stroke. The actual swing should feel easy and rhythmic, similar to a long putt. Some experts advocate that one should pick a spot on the green on which to land the ball when chipping. There are others who visualise the overall picture of the shot; the ball leaving the clubface at the correct loft angle and then landing and running to the hole. Both methods have proved effective, but which-

ever one is used, always remember to keep the head very steady and the eyes on the right-hand side of the ball, when playing these short shots.

Hold for Short Irons

On all of the foregoing shots it is essential to place the hands lower down on the grip of the club. Leave about three inches (7.6 cm) protruding above the left hand, and set the top of the shaft forward until it is level with the front of the ball. This will cause the left wrist to bow slightly towards the target and the back of the right wrist to hollow. It is absolutely essential to maintain both wrists in this position throughout the playing of the stroke. The forward tilting of the top of the shaft with the body weight being distributed with two thirds on the left foot, create the slight downward and forward action required in playing these shots. On no account should the player lean to the right and try to scoop the ball upwards. This is the main cause of two of the cardinal errors frequently committed by players when they are playing delicate shots around the green, namely topping or hitting the ground before contacting the ball.

Summary

In summing up, the player's main objective should be to play the easiest shot possible when dealing with shots from 120 yards (110 m) inwards. Never chip if it is possible to putt and never pitch if it is possible to chip. Always take a good look at the problem before selecting the club and, having done this, visualise the stroke leaving the clubface and making its way to the hole.

Fig 50   A running chip with a 7-iron. Note the
low position of the clubhead, owing to
lack of wrist action.

Fig 51   *The 7-iron chip on its way to the hole.*
Note again the low position of the
clubhead. This shot is almost a putt
with a lofted club.

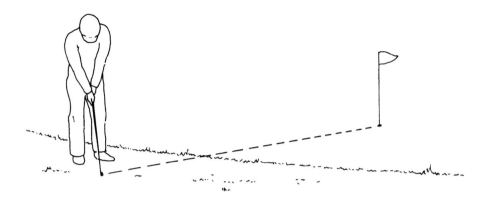

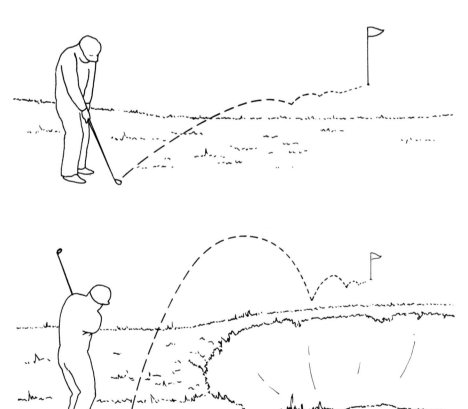

Fig 52   *Never chip if it is possible to putt, and*
never pitch if it is possible to chip.

Fig 53 *Medium iron shot, with the hands ahead of the clubhead just prior to impact.*

MEDIUM IRONS

(Figs 53 to 56)

The 5, 6 and 7-irons are generally considered the most popular clubs. They hit the ball a reasonable distance and are relatively easy to use. In order to ensure consistently accurate striking of the ball with these clubs, the average player would be well advised to play the ball from a point about two inches (5 cm) to the right of a line drawn out from the inside of the left heel to the ball-to-target line. The reason for this is that the club is in its final stages of descent at this point and a slightly descending blow will ensure that the ball will climb to the correct height, relative to the club being used, and that it will have maximum

Fig 54 *A good impact position. Left arm and shaft in line and the body weight moving in the direction of the target.*

backspin. Backspin is essential for accuracy, as it causes the ball to pull up quickly on landing.

The 5-iron is the key club to use when sharpening up one's medium iron play. Neil Coles, who has been one of the most successful tournament players in Britain for the last twenty years, told me that early in his career he hit nothing but 5-iron shots for six months. The reason for this was that he was trying to eliminate an existing fault in his swing and to develop a correctly grooved movement, which could be relied upon to produce solid shots under pressure. One has only to see the quality of his striking, even though he is now in his late forties, to see what a wonderfully repetitive and reliable swing he produced.

Fig 55   *Both arms are now fully extended, just
as they should be immediately after
impact.*

Fig 56   *(overleaf) Greg Norman, just after
impact with a medium iron. Note how
his feet are working correctly to allow
his body to flow in unison with the
swinging arms.*

Fig 57 *The address for a 4-iron. Hands a little nearer the legs than with a wood. All the other factors are virtually the same.*

LONG IRONS *(Figs 57 to 61)*

The 2, 3 and 4-irons are the most difficult irons for the average player. Their longer shafts and lack of loft make consistently solid striking extremely difficult. Most players with handicaps of ten and upwards fare better with the slightly longer shafted but more generously lofted woods, and from my teaching experience I would advise them to use a number 5 wood in preference to a 2 or 3-iron.

There are situations where one might be tempted to suggest that a 2-iron would be better. Against the wind, for example, a well-struck 2-iron shot, with its lower trajectory, would be a safer shot to play than a high-flying shot with the number 5 wood.

Fig 58   *Halfway back with the 4-iron, clubface*
          square. Right elbow starting to fold
          and wrist cocking about to begin.

Technique

A well-struck 2-iron shot can only be produced with the correct technique, developed and consolidated by regular practice with the long irons. The swing is virtually the same as when hitting wood shots. Play the ball from a point opposite the left heel, and sweep the ball away with a square accelerating clubface, travelling from slightly inside the line as it approaches impact, and travelling through the ball towards the target before coming back inwards and upwards.

Fig 59   Completion of the backswing with the 4-iron. Shaft parallel to the ball-to-target line. Left side has responded to the swinging club and arms.

Use a Tee

Do not hesitate to start the practice session by hitting shots off a tee. This will increase the chances of successful shots, and success breeds success. After about twenty shots using the tee, play the remainder from the ground but from good lies.

Fig 60   *Nearing completion of the forward
         swing. Note how the toe of the club is
         pointing towards the sky as a result of
         the forearms rotating naturally with the
         unwinding body.*

Fig 61   *The finish of the 4-iron shot. Virtually
the same as the finish of the swing
with the wood.*

Drop Back to a Middle Iron

If the shots are not too successful with the long irons, it is advisable to drop back to a 5 or 6-iron. This helps to establish confidence and can help to instil a clearer awareness of rhythm. Most bad long iron shots stem from a desire to hit the ball too hard. Remember there are only about ten yards between each club, so try to hit every shot with the same tempo.

FAIRWAY WOODS
(Figs 62 to 67)

Many players experience difficulty with wooden club shots from the turf. This is invariably due to a lack of confidence, arising from one or two disasters in the past. One of the best ways to overcome this fear of fairway woods is to take the most lofted wood in the

Fig 62 *A comfortable address position: arms hanging comfortably with the hands clear of the front of the thighs. Note parallelism of feet and shoulders, and the slightly flexed knees.*

bag to the practice ground, i.e. a number 5 wood or a number 6 wood. Place the ball on a low tee and hit some smooth, easy shots. When they are going well, lower the tee until virtually all of it is in the ground. The fact that there is a tee underneath the ball helps to remove some of the fear. It also tends to make the player swing the club backwards and forwards as opposed to upwards and down-

wards. The latter type of swing will develop if the player practises from bare lies. After a short spell from a tee, the player should place the ball on a nice piece of turf for each shot. This again will encourage the sweeping action which is so essential. Gradually drop down to the number 4 and number 3 woods on these practice sessions. The fear of fairway woods will soon disappear.

Fig 63 *Halfway back with the club pointing directly away from the target. Right elbow beginning to fold and wrist cocking about to begin.*

Shot Making

Fig 64 *Wrists fully cocked with left arm comfortably straight. Shaft parallel to the ball-to-target line. Left shoulder, hip and knee responding to swinging club and arms.*

Fig 65 *Halfway through with the clubshaft parallel to the ball-to-target line. This shows that a correct arc is from in, to straight, to in.*

Fig 66 *A balanced finish with the body facing the target, and the sole of the right shoe looking straight back behind the player. Note the firmness of the hands.*

Only when a reasonable degree of proficiency has been attained from good lies, should the player move on to playing fairway woods from tight bare lies or downslopes. They call for a steeper attack on the ball, which tends to make the club travel from out to in through impact. This type of attack makes the ball travel through the air with a left-to-right spin on it, so aim at a secondary target to the left of the original target.

Never attempt to hook a shot with a fairway wood from a bad lie. The in-to-out shallow attack on the ball required to hook it would tend to make the club strike the ground prior to contacting the ball.

Anyone aspiring to become a better than average golfer must be able to perform competently with fairway woods, so devote quite a bit of practice time to these clubs; it will pay off handsomely.

Fig 67 *A front view of the finish. Note the height of the hands and the position of the elbows, and how the head and eyes have turned to watch the flight of the ball.*

SLOPING LIES

There are very few absolutely level golf courses in the world. Therefore, a player is often required to deal with shots of an unusual nature. This is particularly applicable on links courses where the fairways slope so severely that some of the lies are actually considered

unfair. However, there are ways of dealing with these awkward situations. Realise that you should not try to fight the slopes. Develop an understanding of how they are likely to affect the flight of the ball. The four main situations which occur are:

1. Ball above the feet.
2. Ball below the feet.
3. Ball on an uphill lie.
4. Ball on a downhill lie.

The ball's behaviour in each of these instances is different, and by reading about what to expect and how to deal with it, you will be better equipped to cope with the problems.

Ball Above the Feet
(Figs 69 & 70)

The ball will travel through the air with a hooking flight. This is caused by the swingplane being made flatter than usual as a result of the awkward address position. It is also caused by the fact that a clubface looks more to the left when placed on an upslope. To accommodate the hook, the shot should be aimed at a secondary target to the right of the actual target. Play the ball from opposite the centre of the stance and shorten the hold on the club. Lean into the slope to offset the tendency to fall back during the swing.

Allow the body to turn smoothly to the right and left in unison with the swinging club and arms, and take care that the hands and wrists are not over-active through impact. This would tend to turn the clubface into a closed situation too rapidly and produce a smothered shot.

Fig 68 *(opposite) Tony Jacklin, a former British and US Open Champion, at the completion of a full drive. Note how everything has flowed through to a smoothly balanced finish.*

Fig 69   Ball above the feet. Note the
          shortened hold on the club, and the
          body weight more towards the toes.

Fig 70   *The flatter swing caused by the ball
         being above the feet. This will make
         the ball spin right to left, so aim right to
         allow for this.*

Fig 71 *Ball below the feet. Body weight more towards the heels. The backside is pushed back more than usual to counterbalance the forward bend of the upper body.*

Ball Below the Feet
(Figs 71 & 72)

The ball will travel through the air with a slicing flight. This is caused by the upright plane created by the player having to stand closer to the ball at address, and having to bend forward from the hips more than on a normal lie. Allow for the slice by aiming at a secondary target to the left of the actual target. Play the ball from opposite the inside of the left heel

Fig 72   *A clear view of the more upright swing which occurs when the ball is below the feet. This will cause the ball to spin from left to right, so aim slightly to the left to allow for this.*

and hold the club at full length. Have a feeling of sitting back on the heels during the swing. This will help to offset the tendency to fall towards the ball during the swing, which would cause the strike to be made with the heel of the club. Make a smooth balanced swing at the ball, and emphasise arm and hand action through impact.

Fig 73   An uphill lie. The spine is set at right
angles to the slope, which
encourages the attack on the ball to
travel up the slope through impact.

Ball on an Uphill Lie *(Fig 73)*

The ball will climb higher from an upslope than from level ground, so take a less lofted club than you would normally take to cover the required distance. The spine should be tilted to the right until it is at a right angle to the slope. This will automatically cause the left knee to bend more than the right.

Play the ball from opposite the higher foot and swing mainly with the arms and hands. Because of the left knee being bent more than usual, the turning of the hips through impact will be restricted. This restriction tends to make the hands cross over a little faster at impact, which will tend to hook the ball, so aim a little to the right of the target to allow for this.

Ball on a Downhill Lie *(Fig 74)*

This is considered by most players to be the most difficult of all the sloping lies from which to hit successful shots. The ground behind the ball, being higher, tends to get in the way of the clubhead as it is being swung down towards impact.

There are two ways of overcoming this problem. One method is to hit the ball with a straight flight, by playing it from a point opposite the right foot and setting the spine at a right angle to the slope. This will automatically cause the right knee to bend more than the left. The club selected for this shot should be two clubs more lofted than would normally be required to cover the distance from level ground.

A feeling of swinging the club up the slope on the backswing and down the slope on the forward swing is required. Even with a more lofted club, the ball will travel through the air with a low trajectory and run a considerable distance after it lands, so do not attempt this shot if there are cross bunkers or water hazards in front of the green.

The second method of playing from a down slope is the cut shot. This is played in a similar manner to the greenside bunker shot. The bottom front edge of the clubface is aimed at the target and the ball is played from a point opposite the inside of the left heel. Lines across the feet and shoulders should point about forty-five degrees to the left of the target.

Swing the arms and club parallel to the shoulder line on both the backward and forward swing. Initially the ball will start along the out-to-in swing line, but the open face at impact will cause it to gently curve back on to the target. The latter method is the better when a fairly high quick-stopping shot is required.

Always have one or two practice swings before playing a shot from any sloping lie. This will give the body a feeling of what is required of it during the swing.

DELIBERATE SLICING AND HOOKING

There are numerous situations on a golf course where a player with the ability to play a deliberate slice or hook would have a distinct advantage over a less talented player.

Principles of Spin

Before attempting to put sidespin on the ball, the principles of spin must be clearly understood. If a clubface at impact is looking to the right of the direction in which the clubhead is travelling, it will send the ball through the air with a left-to-right spin, in other words a slice.

Conversely, a clubface which is looking to the left of where the clubhead is travelling, will cause the ball to travel through the air with a right-to-left spin, in other words a hook.

Fig 74   *A downhill lie. The ball is placed further
back in relation to the stance, to
ensure that it is contacted before the
ground.*

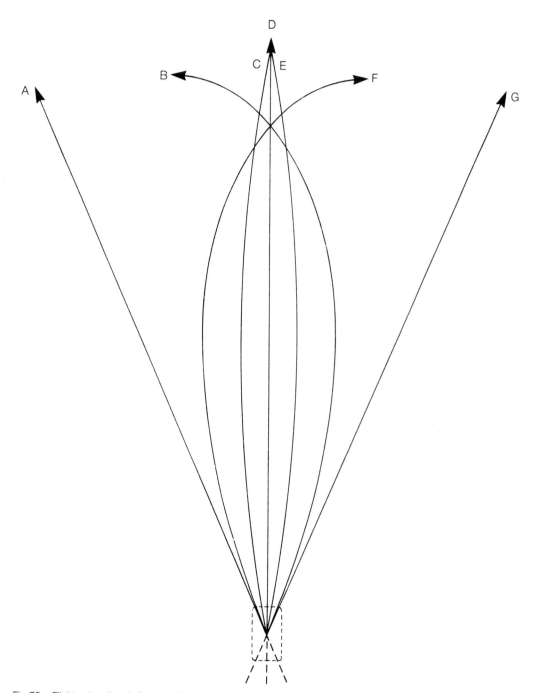

Fig 75   *Flightpaths: A pull; B hook; C fade landing on target; D straight; E draw landing on target; F slice; G push.*

Slice

If the player decides that a slice is required to swerve the ball round some trees, the following procedure must be adopted.

The clubface should be aimed slightly left of the trees and the shoulders and feet should be set open to the clubface. This will encourage an out-to-in attack on the ball through impact, which will set the ball off to the left of where the clubface was originally aimed. As the ball climbs into the air it will start to spin rightwards, which will take it round the trees to its intended target.

Hook

If a hook is required, the clubface should be aimed slightly right of the trees and the shoulders and feet should be set closed to the clubface. This will create an in-to-out attack on the ball which will set the ball off to the right of where it was aimed. As the ball climbs, the hook spin will take over and the ball will travel round the trees to its target. Always remember, aim well clear of the trouble with the clubface at address.

Fade

If a very slight slice has to be applied to the ball, which is called a fade and is often used as a standard method of playing by some top tournament players, the clubface should be aimed very slightly left of the intended target and the shoulders and feet set slightly open to the clubface. This set-up will be sufficient to put the almost imperceptible left-to-right spin on the ball. Lee Trevino, the great American player, is an excellent example of a golfer who uses this type of shot to great effect.

Draw

There are others who play a controlled draw very successfully. Bobby Locke, the South African who won the British Open on four occasions, hit all his shots with a controlled right-to-left spin. This calls for the clubface to be aimed slightly right of the intended target and the feet and shoulders set slightly closed to the clubface.

Note

On all of the foregoing shots, make sure that the clubhead path through the ball is parallel to the shoulders, and do not attempt these shots until they have been practised fairly extensively on the practice ground.

4 Faults

FAULT FINDING

The teaching manual used at the Professional Golfers' Association School at the National Sports Centre in Shropshire, stresses the importance of systematically tracing faults in the swing. The obvious starting point is the clubface, which is the only thing that makes contact with the ball during the making of a stroke. This must be aimed absolutely squarely at the address and returned to this position at impact. In addition to being square at impact, it must be on a path which, if extended, would travel directly to the intended target. The player's positioning of the hands when making the hold will influence the position of the clubface at impact, and the ball position and body and feet alignment will influence the path of the clubhead. A third and most important impact factor, is the angle at which the club approaches the ball prior to and during impact. This should be likened to an aeroplane

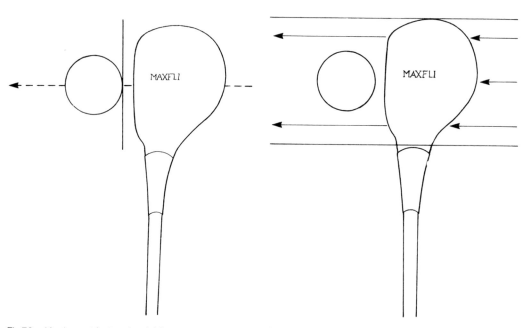

Fig 76   *Key impact factor; the clubface must be square at address.*

Fig 77   *Key impact factor; the clubface must be travelling along the ball-to-target line at impact.*

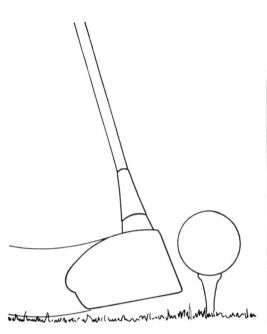

Fig 78   *Key impact factor; the club should contact the ball just after the lowest point in the arc.*

Fig 79   *Too narrow a stance. This would produce very little power.*

landing correctly on an airfield, the descent being neither too steep nor too shallow. This third factor is determined by the player's posture at address. Legs too straight and body bent forward too much will create steepness, and knees too bent and back too vertical will lead to an approach which would be too shallow.

The position of the ball in relation to the left heel must also be checked. Because the clubhead travels in an arc during the swing, there is only a small segment of the arc during which it is actually travelling on the ball-to-target line. This segment runs from approximately the middle of the stance to a point opposite the inside edge of the left foot. Therefore, a ball played to the right of the centre of the stance will be met by a clubface which is travelling and looking slightly rightwards. Conversely, a ball played to the left of the left foot will find the clubface travelling and looking leftwards.

Fig 80   *Too wide a stance. This would prevent the body pivoting naturally in response to the swinging arms.*

It follows that an analysis of what the ball does after being impacted by the club, should convey to the player what the club's impact factors were. For instance, a ball starting to the left of the ball-to-target line and eventually slicing, tells us that the swingpath was to the left and the clubface was open to the swing-path. The cures for this particular pair of faults will be found in the section on slicing. The causes and cures for other common faults are also found under their particular headings.

Fig 81 *Preparing to find the correct width of stance for a drive.*

Fig 82 *Take a normal walking pace with the left foot.*

Summary – Address *(Fig 84)*

1. Square clubface to ball-to-target line.
2. Show two and a half to three knuckles on left hand and make sure that the vees on both hands point to the right shoulder.
3. Parallel shoulders and feet to ball-to-target line.
4. Flex knees and keep spinal column straight – tilt slightly forward from hips – just enough to place base of club lightly on the ground with the centre of the clubface behind the centre of the ball.
5. Make sure that the left arm is comfortably straight with the butt end of the hand hanging about four or five inches (10–12.5 cm) clear of the left thigh. The right arm should be slightly bent with the bone of the elbow looking at the right hip.
6. Feel that the right shoulder is set in and under the left – try to reproduce this feeling at impact.

Fig 83 *Turn body and feet through ninety degrees and lower the club to the ground. This is the ideal width.*

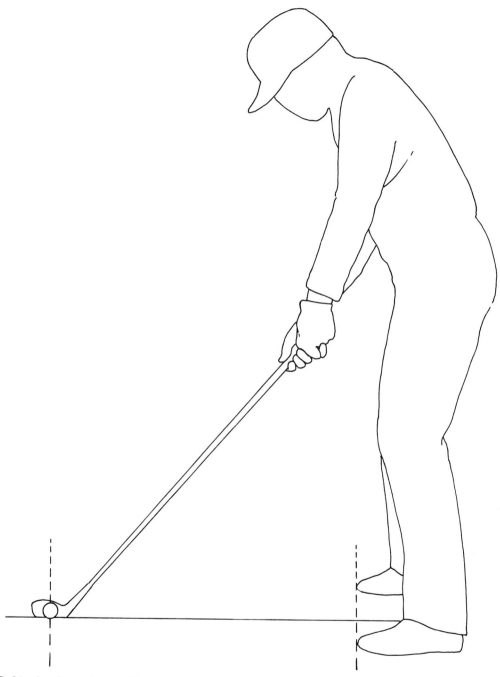

Fig 84   A perfect address position; arms
          hanging clear of the body and knees
          slightly flexed. Feet and shoulders
          parallel to the ball-to-target line.

Faults

Summary – The Swing
(Fig 85)

1. Make sure that the clubface remains square to the arc of the swing as it starts its backward journey.
2. Turn shoulders and hips and move left knee inwards in unison with the swinging arms.
3. Make sure that the left thumb and right wrist are under the shaft at the top of the backswing.
4. Start down with arms and left knee working in unison.
5. Swing clubhead freely and strongly through impact.
6. Finish with hips and shoulders turned through to face the target with body weight balanced on the outside edge of the left foot.

Reminder – the above summaries relate to right-handed players. If you are left-handed, for right read left and vice versa.

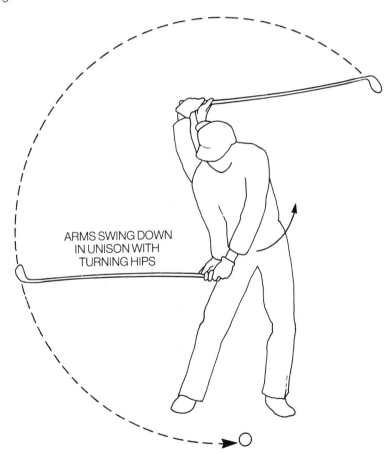

ARMS SWING DOWN
IN UNISON WITH
TURNING HIPS

Fig 85   *The correct downswing sequence, lower body moving left as arms swing downwards.*

SLICING

Causes

Slicing is caused by the face of the club being open at impact. This can be created by the player having either one or both hands too much to the left when addressing the ball. It can also happen if the player's forearms and hands are turning clockwise through the impact zone.

The automatic reaction to a slice is to aim further left to accommodate it. Doing this actually increases the amount of slice spin on the ball, and the length of the shot is considerably less than it should be, relative to the club being used.

Cures

Check the aim from behind the ball as advised in the section on addressing the ball. Set the clubface correctly behind the ball with the bottom front edge square to ball-to-target line. Firstly, hold the club with the left hand and check that approximately two and a half to three of the knuckles at the base of the fingers are visible and that the vee formed between the thumb and forefinger points to the right shoulder. The right hand should then take its place on the grip and, irrespective of which of the three holds the player uses, the palm of the hand should face in exactly the opposite direction to the left.

The club should be held in the fingers, and the vee formed between the thumb and forefinger should point to the right shoulder, exactly parallel to the vee of the left hand.

Having aimed and made the hold, the player must ensure that the lines across the feet and shoulders are parallel to the ball-to-target line. Ball position and stance width are also very critical. The back of the ball should be opposite the inside of the left heel, and the distance between the insides of the heels should be approximately the same as the width of the shoulders. Make sure that the stance does not become too wide as this tends to restrict the body's pivoting action.

Always remember when trouble sets in, check through the basics of aim, hold, ball position, alignment and posture before starting to tamper with the swing.

During the actual swing, the player should ensure that on the initial takeaway from the ball the clubhead travels straight back from the ball for only ten to twelve inches (25–30 cm). From that point on, it should curve inwards and upwards and finish up parallel to the ball-to-target line when the shoulders have completed their ninety degree turn. On the downswing, make sure that the right elbow drops closely into the side as the reversing action from backswing to downswing takes place.

Another important feeling that the player should acquire, is that of making the clubhead travel back into the ball along the same path as it travelled on its journey away from the ball. After impact, allow both forearms to turn naturally to the left as the clubhead is released freely through the ball. Make sure that the hips and shoulders turn completely through to look squarely at the target at the end of the stroke, and that the sole of the right shoe is turned so that it looks directly away from the target.

PULLING

Causes

In the same way that pushing and slicing seem to be connected, pulling and hooking are considered by some players to be of the same origin.

The pull actually belongs to the out-to-in family, and the only difference between the pull and the slice is the position of the clubface at impact. In the pulled shot it is square, and in the sliced shot it is open to the out-to-in path.

The two main causes are, having the ball too far to the left of the left foot at address, and swinging the clubhead on an arc outside the correct path on the downswing, prior to impact.

Cures

Check all basics as usual, particularly the ball position in relation to the left heel. Make sure that the arms and left knee start the down-swing. This assists in delivering the club from the inside.

Always try to drive the square clubface through the ball in the direction of a front marker, which should be selected before aiming the clubface at address. Also, make sure that the gentle inward curve described by the clubhead soon after takeaway is retraced by the clubhead on its forward swing into and through the ball.

HOOKING

Causes

Hooking is a fault which affects good players much more than slicing. The cause is exactly opposite to that of the slice, in that the hook is caused by a closed clubface. This can stem

Fig 86   *A typical slicer's stance; an open stance, with everything aimed to the left of the target.*

Fig 87   *The result of an open stance; the clubshaft is pointing well left of the target. This will produce a slice or, occasionally, a pull.*

Fig 88   *A typical hooker's stance; a closed stance, with everything aimed to the right of the target.*

Fig 89   *The result of the closed stance; the clubshaft is pointing well to the right of the target. This will produce a hook or, occasionally, a push.*

from the fact that either one or both hands are turned too much to the right when addressing the ball. This encourages the forearms and hands to turn anticlockwise too quickly through impact.

The player automatically reacts to the hook by aiming well to the right, which increases the amount of hook spin on the ball, as this type of alignment creates an in-to-out swing path.

Cures

Check through the basics in the correct sequence exactly as recommended in the section on slicing. Most faulty shots occur because the player is not adhering to these basics. Read through the section on how to play a fade and a heavy slice, and apply some of these principles. In other words, take a slight overdose of the prescribed cure.

PUSHING

Causes

Many players fail to distinguish the difference between a shot which is pushed and one which is sliced. This is probably because they both finish up on the right-hand side of the course.

The push, in fact, belongs to the in-to-out family and is a blood brother of the hook. The only difference is that the clubface is square to the path when the ball is pushed and closed to the path when the ball is hooked. The two main causes are the ball being placed too far to the right of the left heel at address, and the swing arc being too flat.

Cures

Again it must be back to the basics of aim, hold, ball position, alignment, posture, in the

93

address.

In the actual swing, feel that the club starts straight back for ten to twelve inches (25–30 cm) and returns to deliver a square blow along that line. Setting the maker's name on the back centre of the ball when teeing it up, helps the player to concentrate on the above impact thought.

Another useful aid to eliminating the problem is to pick up a front marker about four or five yards (or metres) in front of the ball on the target line, and make a determined effort to strike the ball over this point. Check also that a line drawn along the back of the ball would run along the inside edge of the left heel.

TOPPING

Causes

Believe it or not, one of the main causes of topping the ball is trying to keep one's head down too much. Many experienced players pass this 'head down' theory on to their less talented friends as though it was the panacea for all golfing ills.

Ideally, the player should address the ball with the eyes down and the head slightly up, the chin held clear of the chest. This allows the shoulders to turn and tilt at right angles to the upper portion of the spine. If the head is held too low with the chin tight to the chest, the shoulders will merely tilt. This causes a very steep action which will make the player hit the ground before the ball. After a few disasters of this nature, the player reacts by pulling the upper body upwards at impact, which produces the topped shot.

There are many other causes of topping, most of them stemming from an incorrect address position. Stretching for the ball by standing too far away at address, and failure to flex the knees are two other common causes of topping. Holding the club too tightly at address, which causes overall tension in the body is another. Positioning the ball too much to the left will also cause topping, as the club is beginning to ascend into the follow-through at this point in the swing.

Cures

To cure topping go back to the section on addressing the ball and check all basics. During the actual stroke watch the ball being struck by the clubface and maintain the address spinal angle throughout the swing. Make sure that the wrists are allowed to uncock naturally as they enter the hitting area.

FLUFFING

Causes

Fluffing is the term used to describe the situation in which the club hits the ground prior to contacting the ball. This is a common fault, and a very irritating one as it robs the shot of its correct length.

The fault can often be traced to an incorrect set-up. Standing too near the ball at address is a common cause. Another is crouching too much, which tends to create an up and down body movement during the swing. Even when the set-up is correct, players are prone to fluffing shots because of an incorrect swing sequence. Picking the club up at the start of the backswing, instead of a one-piece takeaway, will steepen the arc too severely and thus cause a fluff.

Failure to move the left knee and hips laterally at the start of the downswing can also produce the fault. The latter will tend to produce an early uncocking of the wrists, which will widen the arc and deliver the club several inches behind the ball.

Cures

1. Measure off correctly, with the clubshaft plus a comfortably straight left arm, and the butt end of the hand about four or five inches (10–12.5 cm) from the inside of the left thigh.
2. Flex the knees slightly and keep the chin off the chest, eyes down and head up.
3. Keep the head comfortably steady throughout the swing.
4. Check that the ball position relative to the club being used is correct. It sometimes creeps forward without the player realising it.
5. Make sure that the left knee flexion created at address is not greater at impact.
6. Delay the release of the hands until the correct moment on the downswing.

SHANKING OR SOCKETING *(Fig 90)*

Causes

Shanking, or socketing as it is sometimes called, is one of golf's most dreaded faults. This is a shot which is struck with the base of the socket into which the shaft is fitted on irons. The ball shoots off to the right at about forty-five degrees to the intended line. Naturally, the player thinks that the swing-path must be out-to-in because the ball behaves as though it has been sliced. In fact, the opposite swing-path, in-to-out, is one of the main causes of this dreaded disease.

It has been said that some teaching professionals refuse to try to cure a victim for fear of developing the problem themselves. Personally, I find this hard to believe, and am perfectly happy to help any player rid himself of the problem. In fact, I often demonstrate the low socket and the high socket on golf clinics.

Fig 90   *A socket; the ball has been struck by the tube into which the shaft is fitted, and is setting off low at a tangent of about forty-five degrees.*

Knowing how to do it makes it easier for me to cure it.

I have already said that swinging too much from in-to-out can create the problem, but another cause is swinging in a correct arc going back, but then coming outside the true arc on the downswing. This puts the centre of the clubface about one inch (25 mm) beyond the ball and the contact is made with the socket.

Faults

Cures

1. Check all address factors, keeping to the system outlined in the chapter on addressing the ball.
2. Place a fairly long white tee about one and a half inches (4 cm) to the right of the ball and another about ten to twelve inches (25–30 cm) behind the ball on an extension of the ball-to-target line.
3. Keep the face of the club square, and swing the back of the club towards the tee behind the ball. Complete the backswing and strike down and through the ball, leaving the tee close to the ball standing in the ground.

4. During the downswing, make sure that the body weight does not go onto the toes, and try to keep the angle of spinal tilt constant throughout the swing. An easy way to achieve this is to feel that the distance from the chin to the ball remains exactly the same until after impact, where the head turns and rises into the correct finish.

Instead of placing a tee close to the ball to check the swing-path, I sometimes use a car washing sponge. This helps the player to visualise the correct swing-path, and does not damage the club if the swing is outside the path.

5 Coaching

HOW I TEACH BEGINNERS

A golf swing must be built to last and, like anything else which requires such a criterion, solid foundations are essential. No beginner should be introduced to the full golf swing at the outset. It is much wiser to take them to the edge of a putting green and explain the principles of the running chip.

Fundamentals

Having explained the importance of aim, hold, ball position, alignment and posture, demonstrate the stroke. I tell the pupil to imagine that the hands are at six o'clock on a clock face, and that they should be swung back to seven o'clock and through to five o'clock, stressing that the sole of the club should brush the grass at the start of the backswing, and that the arc described by the club on its forward swing should be a retrace of the backswing arc. Again, the brushing should be felt, this time starting at impact and travelling close to the grass for four to six inches (10–15 cm).

I point out that the only way to produce successful and predictable shots, is to ensure that the clubface is square at impact, that the path of the clubhead travels along the ball-to-target line, and that the base of the club is brushing the surface on which the ball is resting. I tell the pupil to murmur phrases to themselves like "back and through" or "brush and brush". These help to develop the pendulum type action and correct rhythm required for the shot. As the pupils' ability to play this shot gradually develops, they are asked to extend the backswing and through-swing from eight to four and then nine to three on the imaginary clockface.

The pupil is then given some exercises to do. Trunk turning with two clubs across the back is excellent for training the body to turn correctly in both directions. Swinging two long irons backwards and forwards will also instil correct body action and strengthen the hands and arms.

When the pupils are showing control over the swinging club, allow them to take a full backswing and full down and through-swing as described in Chapter 2. Keep to relatively easy clubs initially – 7-iron, 5-iron and then the number 4 wood. I tell the pupils not to be too proud to use a tee at first. This will increase their chances of hitting successful shots and, as in other spheres of activity, success breeds success.

Progressing

When the pupils can hit shots fairly consistently, they are given lessons on pitching, putting and bunker play. As soon as these shots are being played reasonably satisfactorily, the pupils then play a few holes under my guidance. Normally, the first few attempts at playing round the course with only one ball are not too successful. This is quite normal, and practice and perseverance will be required to overcome this difficult barrier.

Ideally, the beginner should have approximately twelve lessons, the first four or five close together to get a quick and clear understanding of the correct fundamentals. The lessons should then be spread out to ten to twelve day intervals with plenty of practice between them. After two or three months' practice and playing, the pupils are recommended to have periodic check-ups to ensure that no serious faults are creeping in. All of the foregoing may seem very much like hard work, but I can assure you that it is time and money well spent. After all, we intend to go on playing golf for a long time, and the solid foundations laid at the beginning will ensure that we will play to a reasonably high standard for the rest of our golfing lives.

ESTABLISHED PLAYERS

When a more experienced player arrives for a lesson I always ask them what they think their problem is. I then ask them what their handicap is, and how long they have been playing golf. From their answers I form a quick opinion as to how much they know about the game.

Analysis

I then ask them to hit some shots with a number 6 or 7-iron. As the shots are being hit, I stand in front of them for a short time to check the manner in which they hold the club, and the position of the ball relative to their left heel. I then move round to a point directly behind the ball-to-target line. This enables me to check their aim, alignment and posture. It also discloses the path of the clubhead on the backswing and downswing.

Keeping in mind that the pupil has already told me what they think their problem is, I watch the behaviour of the ball to see if they have made a correct analysis.

They are often wrong, and have thought that a pull caused by an out-to-in swing was a hook. This can cause the ball to hook if the face is closed at impact, but generally speak-

ing an out-to-in swing will cause a straight pull, particularly with lofted clubs. My next move is to show the pupil why the ball is travelling left and then demonstrate the correction.

Correcting

This may involve correcting faults such as having the shoulders too open at address, the ball too much to the left, or the right shoulder moving out and over the left at the start of the downswing. The first two points are relatively easy for the pupil to correct as everything is at rest in the address position. The last fault, the shoulder rolling, always proves more difficult to cure. A feeling of swinging in and under with the right shoulder has to be prescribed, and the pupil encouraged to feel that the clubhead is swinging from inside the line as it approaches the ball, to slightly outside the line after impact. Naturally, this would cause a slight push rather than a straight shot but this I feel is what the pupil must strive for initially to rid themselves of their out-to-in problem. Sometimes several lessons are required to cure this, and only by practising assiduously between lessons can the pupil eventually develop the correct in-to-straight-through swingpath which, coupled with a square face, will produce ball-to-target shots.

All other faults are dealt with in the same systematic manner, starting with a thorough check of all the fundamentals, and followed by an explanation of the fault and how to go about curing it. Then follows a demonstration of the fault and the method required to cure it, and from the explanation and demonstration one hopes that the pupil will apply the cure.

Practice Sessions

I always try to impress upon a pupil the importance of some quiet practice sessions following a lesson. So many people rush straight onto the course immediately after a lesson, play badly, and condemn the teacher for having ruined their swing. After all, very few people emerge from a doctor's surgery instantly cured of their ailments.

The most important things, in my opinion, are that the pupil understands what I am talking about and that they are not given more than two things to work on during and after a lesson. In many instances there are five or six evident faults, but to try to get anyone to think of all these at once and hit a golf ball, would prove physically impossible.

Fig 91   *The legs are far too rigid. This tends to create a lifting action instead of a backward swinging action.*

ADVICE FOR THE OVER FIFTIES

Many older golfers ask me why golf professionals don't write books and articles offering advice for people whose games are deteriorating because of old age. As I am now in my fifties myself, I know exactly what they mean. The loss of length from the tee, the inability to hole the short putts with any degree of certainty, that exhausted feeling at the end of thirty-six holes in a day, are all part of the ageing process. We can help to offset this by doing such exercises as trunk turning with two clubs behind the back, and also swinging a heavy training club regularly. Both these exercises will help to arrest the loss of length.

Play regularly, and without long intervals between games, as this will help to keep the body and legs in good condition. Practise the short game more than the long game; this is the area where shots can so easily be wasted through lack of concentration or nervousness as one gets older.

See your professional and seek his advice on shaft flex; you may be using one which is too rigid. The majority of professionals fit more flexible shafts to their clubs when they pass the fifty mark. It is also wise to add a lofted wood to your set, a number 5 or 6, and drop the 2 and 3-irons. The woods are easier to use.

Check through your golf bag regularly, and see that you are not carrying things you do not need. Over a period of time we tend to stuff all sorts of things into the ball pockets and clothing pockets, and end up carrying or pulling a great deal of unnecessary weight.

Finally, go to your professional and have a lesson occasionally, particularly when you run into a bad patch. Many older golfers think that their knowledge and experience will enable them to put things right. This is very seldom the case, as players cannot actually see themselves, whereas the trained eye of the teaching professional can spot the problem and restore the player to golfing health.

Fig 92   *The last three fingers of the left hand have released their hold on the club. This leads to inconsistency in your shots.*

6 Practice and Fitness

PRACTISING CONSTRUCTIVELY

The expression 'practice makes perfect' is not wholly accurate as far as golf is concerned. There are thousands of golfers who have practised a tremendous amount and have not shown the slightest bit of improvement, principally because their methods were so faulty that, no matter how much time they spent hitting balls, the result would always be miserable failure. My advice to anyone who decides to spend a great deal of time on the practice ground in order to become a better player is, go to a qualified teacher and get your method thoroughly checked. By doing this, practice will then prove very beneficial.

There are various forms of practice, from the beginner learning to move the club, arms and body in a reasonably co-ordinated manner, to the top tournament professional honing his game to the highest level of perfection. In between these two groups are what we normally regard as the average player. It is this group to whom I will aim my advice, and the other two groups can extract from this some ideas which will prove beneficial to them.

Analyse Your Game

The first thing the player seeking improvement should do is to analyse their overall game and decide which is the weakest part of it. This should be practised regularly until it becomes the strongest part. Psychologically this can make a tremendous difference to a player. For instance, a player who is scared of playing pitch shots over bunkers, suddenly becoming confident in this department of the game, approaches the whole thing in a different light. The same applies to the poor bunker player, the poor long iron player or the poor driver of the ball. Eliminate your weakness and make it your strength.

Another important point is, practise with reasonable golf balls and put an identification mark on them with a felt-tipped marker. There is nothing more infuriating than finding one of your fellow golfers hitting old cut balls down the practice ground and then collecting your nice clean balls with no cuts on them. By marking them clearly you can help to prevent this.

Tips for the Practice Session

Do not hit too many balls at a time, perhaps about thirty, particularly when working on full shots with woods or long irons. Then go and collect them; this gives your body and your mind a bit of a rest.

If you still have some energy left, hit another thirty, collect the balls and finish the session off by going to the putting green for half an hour. Always try to fit in some putting practice every time you visit the course for any practice session. Being a good putter is probably the greatest psychological booster of all.

As the proficiency factor increases, try to simulate on-course situations when practising. Imagine you are driving on a left to right dog-leg hole, and try to fade the ball round the corner, or imagine there is a strong right to left wind blowing and you are going to aim right and put a touch of draw on the shot. This will help to teach shot visualisation, and make practising more interesting and productive.

WARMING UP

Warming up before a round is somewhat different from normal practice. This should consist of hitting about six balls with each of the even numbered or odd numbered clubs as a means of establishing rhythm and loosening the muscles.

Always start with the short irons and work up through the clubs to the driver. It is always advisable to hit the last three or four balls with the club with which you intend to be hitting your first tee shot – a sort of final dress rehearsal.

Unfortunately, very few players spend any time warming up, but I feel sure that it would help to eliminate many of the disasters which crop up on the early holes. Try it some time; if the top professionals have to do it and most of them play every day, then there is even more need for the man who only plays once or twice a week to do it.

GOLF EXERCISES

Golf may not demand as high a standard of fitness as many of the more active pursuits like squash, tennis, rugby, football or athletics. Nevertheless, being generally fit and supple helps one to play better. There are several simple exercises which, if done regularly, can help a player to become fitter and more supple.

Legs

Obviously, the legs are vitally important as we use them to cover the miles we have to travel during a round of golf. They are also used as

co-ordinating factors during the swing. Therefore, any form of leg exercise will prove beneficial, such as jogging, running on the spot, skipping or playing a few holes by oneself and walking twice as quickly as usual between shots.

Hands, Wrists and Arms
(Figs 94 to 96)

The hands, wrists and arms are vital components in the swing. The hands are the only link with the club, and the arm and wrist action are both absolutely vital in creating the correct plane and for transmitting power.

One of the finest exercises for keeping these parts in top condition is to swing an old wooden headed club, weighted up to about twenty ounces (550 grams). Make sure it has a good grip on it, and take it into the back garden and swing it regularly. If you do not have a heavy swinging club, two or three long irons can serve the same purpose. The main advantage of the single heavy club is the fact that the proper hold can be practised.

Body Action (Figs 97 to 99)

Correct body action can also be practised with the heavy club or the two or three long irons. Place either across the upper part of the back and hold in position with the insides of the elbows. The address position should now be assumed and with the head held steady and the eyes fixed on an imaginary ball on the ground, the body should be rotated smoothly to the right and then to the left – a ninety degree turn to the right followed by a one hundred and eighty degree turn to the left. The emphasis should be on keeping one's head and spine steady, and turning smoothly in each direction.

Fig 93   *(opposite) Severiano Ballesteros, the 1979 and 1984 British Open Champion. This is the swing of a fit young man; the shoulders have turned through more than ninety degrees, and the left heel is still on the ground.*

Fig 94 *Preparing for the swinging exercise with two long irons. This exercise is good for arms and hands, and can help the player to acquire good rhythm.*

Fig 95 *Completion of the backswing. Note how the body has responded to the swinging arms and clubs.*

Fig 96 *End of the swing. The body has turned completely through to face the target. Note also hands to the left of and above the head.*

Fig 97 *Trunk turning exercise. Note that the heads of the two clubs are protruding from the left side; this ensures a good wind up to the right.*

Fig 98 *Shoulders and clubs have turned through ninety degrees. The left eye is fixed on an imaginary ball between the feet.*

Fig 99 *The body has now turned fully round into the follow-through position.*

Hands (Fig 100)

Another excellent exercise for strengthening the hands and developing clubface control, is writing one's name and address in block letters with the head of a sand-iron. Standing with the feet about twelve inches (30 cm) apart, hold the club in front of the body at chest level. The actual describing of the letters by the clubhead is, in effect, a brain to hands to clubhead movement, and as Henry Cotton, one of Britain's greatest players claims, that phrase more or less sums up golf.

Hand Curling

There is also an exercise which is widely used by young professionals, and it is known as hand curling. This can be done by getting a piece of wood about a foot (30 cm) long – a piece of old broom handle is ideal. Drill a hold in the centre, and pass a piece of string about four feet (1.2 m) long through the hole. Tie a knot in the string to prevent it slipping through the handle, and tie the other end to a practice ball bag, half full of balls. With the palms facing downwards, hold the handle and wind the bag up until it almost touches the hands, then wind it back down again to the ground.

This should only be done three times in each direction to begin with, as it puts a severe strain on the hands and forearms. After a spell the number of curls can gradually be increased to six times in each direction. The number of balls in the bag can be increased or decreased according to the player's physical strength.

Fig 100   *The sand-iron set in the position from which the name and address of the player can be written in block letters. An excellent exercise for strengthening the hands and wrists.*

Practice and Fitness

Swinging

Finally, an exercise which is invaluable for building up the feeling of swinging the club mainly with the hands and arms. Take a 7 or 8-iron, and hit shots with the feet together, from good lies. This teaches rhythm, balance and hand action, all of them absolutely essential factors when it comes to playing good golf.

Playing golf to get fit is important, but it is even more important to get fit to play golf!

Fig 101   *Preparation for the one-handed swing with a sand-iron. Note the correct position of the left hand on the club; thumb slightly right of centre, and vee pointing to the right shoulder.*

Fig 102   *Top of the backswing; left thumb
under the shaft, and clubface in an
orthodox square position.*

Fig 103   *Completion of the swing. Left thumb
under the shaft, and back of the left
hand and clubface looking directly
away from the target.*

QUESTIONS AND ANSWERS

Question   Should a lady golfer use men's clubs?

Answer   Many of the leading lady players do use men's clubs with regular shafts. After all, they are only half an inch longer per club and the swingweight is only two or three points higher. Tall, strong lady golfers should definitely use men's clubs.

Question   How tightly should one hold the club?

Answer   Firmly enough to control it, but lightly enough to be aware of the clubhead.

Question   Should the wrists be cocked consciously on the backswing?

Answer   No, this will happen automatically unless the hold pressure is too tight or too loose.

Question   Which part of the game should be practised most?

Answer   The short game, particularly putting.

Question   Should the sand-iron always be used for bunker shots around the green?

Answer   Not necessarily, the pitching wedge or 9-iron are more effective when the sand is very wet or hard packed.

Question   Why does a number three wood hit the ball straight, but the number one wood of the same set tend to slice it?

Answer   Because of the loft on the number three wood, the ball is contacted below its equator and the backspin overrides any sidespin. The reverse occurs with the straighter faced number one wood.

Question   Is a surlyn-covered ball better than a balata-covered ball?

Answer   This depends on the standard of the player. For the expert, the balata-covered ball is better, as it stops quicker after landing, thereby giving better control. The surlyn-covered ball runs more after landing but is much more durable and is recommended for the less skilful player, as it does not cut easily when topped.

Question   Is grip thickness important?

Answer   Yes, grips which are too thin tend to create a wristy swing, and grips which are too thick have the opposite effect.

Question   Is it advisable to pitch with a sand-iron?

Answer   Yes, providing the ball is being played from a good lie.

Question   Is a left-hand glove essential?

Answer   Not absolutely, but there must be some advantage in it, as most of the leading players wear one except for putting. The main advantage is that the feel on the club's grip is constant, whether the hand is hot and sticky or cold and dry.

Question   What makes some players hit the ball much further than others?

Answer   Clubhead speed, squarely applied. Build and physical strength are important factors, and golf exercises can be done to improve the latter.

Question   Is it advisable to choose heavy clubs?

Answer   No, they reduce the potential clubhead speed and make the player feel tired towards the end of a round.

Practice and Fitness

Question What is the best age for a child to start having golf lessons?

Answer About ten years of age. Before that they are not really strong enough or sufficiently interested to pay much attention to a teacher.

Question Is practising more important than playing?

Answer They are both important. After playing, a player should practise whichever department of his/her game was weakest.

Glossary

Address   The position of the player at the ball prior to making the swing.

Air Shot   A complete miss.

Angle of Attack   The angle at which the clubhead approaches the ball on the forward swing.

Approach Shots   Shots to a green from about one hundred and fifty yards (137 metres) inwards.

Apron   The grassy area surrounding the green which is normally cut to a length slightly shorter than the fairway, but slightly longer than the green.

Better-ball Match   A match in which two players play against another two players, and only the better score of each side counts.

Birdie   A score of one stroke under par on a hole.

Blind Hole   A hole where the player cannot see the green or the flagstick when playing an approach shot.

Bogey   One stroke over par on a hole.

Borrow   The amount a player should allow for a putt to move sidewards on a sideslope.

Carry   Tne length which the ball travels from where it is struck to where it lands.

Casual Water   A temporary accumulation of water which is not normally defined as a water hazard.

Chip Shot   A low running approach shot.

Close Lie   A ball lying tight to the ground's surface.

Closed Face   Clubface aimed left of the correct position either at the address or during the actual swing.

Closed Stance   The left foot closer to the ball-to-target line than the right.

Closed Alignment   The left side of the body closer to the ball-to-target line than the right side.

Clubface   The striking surface of the club.

Course Rating   The score a scratch golfer should make when playing well under normal conditions.

Cup   The lining inside the hole, normally made of metal or plastic.

Divot   A piece of turf removed by the club-head when swinging.

Double Bogey   Two strokes over par on a hole.

Down   The number of holes a player or side is behind during a match.

Dormie   Where a player or side is ahead during a match by as many holes as remain to be played.

Draw   A ball curving slightlv from right to left through the air.

Glossary

Drive Shot made with a driver (no. 1 wood) when playing from the teeing ground.

Drop Holding the arm in front of the body at shoulder height with the palm of the hand downwards and dropping the ball when allowed or required to do so by the Rules of Golf.

Duck Hook A shot that curves violently to the left with very little height on it.

Eagle A hole played in two strokes under par.

Fade A shot that moves slightly from left to right through the air.

Fairway The area between the teeing ground and the green, which is regularly mown.

Flagstick The marker in the hole on the green.

Follow-through The part of the swing which occurs after impact.

Fourball A match in which two players play their better ball against the better ball of another two players.

Foursome A match in which two players play against another two players, each side using one ball and playing alternate shots.

Front Nine The first nine holes of a course.

Green The closely mown area on which the hole is cut.

Grip The material on the shaft on to which the player places his hands.

Gross Score The player's score for a round with no handicap deduction.

Halve To complete a hole in the same score as the opposition in match-play.

Handicap An adjustable figure awarded to players according to their scoring ability against the standard scratch score of a course.

Hazards Natural or man-made areas filled with sand or water, in which the club cannot be grounded when addressing the ball.

Hook A shot which curves violently from right to left.

Inside-out The clubhead travelling from inside the ball-to-target line to outside it through the impact zone.

Lie The angle formed by the shaft and the sole of the club. Also used to describe the ball's position.

Match-play Where the result is decided by holes with match-play rules being applied.

Medal Play Where the player's score is recorded at each hole and totalled up at the end of the round, also known as stroke play.

Open Face Clubface looking to the right of the target at address or impact. Also used to describe the face position in relation to the swing arc during the swing.

Open Stance Where the right foot is closer to the ball-to-target line than the left at address.

Outside-in The clubhead travelling from outside to inside the ball-to-target line through impact.

Par The score a first-class player is expected to achieve on a hole allowing two putts on the green.

Pitch A high approach shot made with a 9-iron, pitching wedge or sand wedge.

Plugged Ball A ball which remains in its own indentation when landing on soft ground.

Preferred Lies Where players are allowed to place the ball on the fairways during the winter months or when the fairways are in poor condition.

Pull A shot which travels straight through the air but to the left of the target. Caused by the club's swingpath being out-to-in.

Push The exact opposite of the pull. Caused by the club's swingpath being in-to-out.

Rough Anywhere that is not maintained and cut as a tee, fairway, green or hazard.

Scratch Competition A competition in which only the gross scores count.

Shaft Flex The amount by which a shaft is designed to bend. Shafts can be obtained in different degrees of flexibility.

Shank A shot struck on the inside part of the hosel on an iron club, also known as a socket.

Sky To go too much underneath the ball at impact, and consequently send it much higher than normal.

Slice A shot which swerves violently from

left to right, caused by an open clubface at impact.

Sole The bottom part of the club. Also used to describe the act of placing the club behind the ball when squaring the clubface to the ball-to-target line.

Square Stance When both feet are equidistant from the ball-to-target line; it is also important to ensure that the body lines agree with the line across the toes.

Stroke Forward movement of the club made with the intention of striking the ball.

Swingweight A measurement used to match clubs to each other so that they feel the same when swung. Most golf shops have a swingweight machine for checking clubs.

Takeaway The start of the backswing.

Target Line The line connecting the ball and the target.

Texas Wedge An imported expression from the United States. It describes a shot played with a putter from off the green.

Through the Green The area between the tee and the green, excepting hazards.

Top When the bottom front edge of the clubface contacts the ball above its equator.

Vardon Grip Named after the famous player Harry Vardon who is supposed to have originated the overlap grip.

Waggle A smooth fluid backward and forward movement of the club at address, created by the wrists only.

Useful Addresses

English Golf Union
1–3 Upper King Street
Leicester LE1 6XF

English Ladies' Golf Association
PO Box 14
52 Boroughgate
Otley
West Yorkshire LS21 1QW

Royal and Ancient Golf Club
St Andrews
Fife KY16 9JD

The Professional Golfers' Association
Wentworth Club
Wentworth Drive
Virginia Water
Surrey GU25 4LS

Scottish Golf Union
The Cottage
181a Whitehouse Road
Barnton
Edinburgh EH4 6BY

Welsh Golf Union
2 Isfryn
Burry Port
Dyfed SA16 0BY

Golfing Union of Ireland
Glencar House
81 Eglinton Road
Donnybrook
Dublin 4

The Ladies' Golf Union
12 The Links
St Andrews
Fife

Scottish Ladies' Golfing Association
1 Trinity Place
St Andrews
Fife

Welsh Ladies' Golf Union
Ysgoldy Gynt
Llanhennock
Newport
Gwent NP6 1LT

Irish Ladies' Golf Union
44 Maretimo Gardens
E. Blackrock
Co. Dublin